SUETONIUS
NERO

Edited with Introduction,
Notes and Bibliography by

B.H. Warmington

Second Edition

Bristol Classical Press

This impression 2003
This edition published in 1977 by
Bristol Classical Press
an imprint of
Gerald Duckworth & Co. Ltd.
90-93 Cowcross Street, London EC1M 6BF
Tel: 020 7490 7300
Fax: 020 7490 0080
inquiries@duckworth-publishers.co.uk
www.ducknet.co.uk

A catalogue record for this book is available
from the British Library

ISBN 1 85399 541 X

Printed and bound in Great Britain by
Antony Rowe Ltd, Eastbourne

Contents

Preface to the 1999 Edition

After some twenty years of useful life, the format of the 1977 edition has become obsolete, and this new edition has been entirely reset. The opportunity has been taken to make a number of revisions and additions to the notes. In the intervening years our understanding of Suetonius has been advanced by the works of A. Wallace-Hadrill and B. Baldwin, of the *Nero* by the Commentary of K.R. Bradley, and of the principate of Nero by M.T.Griffin (see the Bibliography for details). I have not normally engaged in scholarly dialogue with these and other recent authors in the notes, though obviously differences in interpretation will be found. I am grateful to Donald Hill for additional notes compiled by him in the course of teaching with this text, some of which have been used or adapted.

B.H. Warmington
Hartland, Devon

Preface to the First Edition

This edition of Suetonius' *Nero* is designed primarily for students in schools and universities to read as an important example of Latin biography and as a major source for some of the most dramatic events in the history of the first century AD. The notes are almost all devoted to the explanation of historical points in the text, the elucidation of Suetonius' approach to the principate of Nero, and a comparison of his version of events with those found in the other authors who cover the same period of history. I have accordingly indicated parallel references in Tacitus and Dio wherever appropriate, though I am conscious that completeness in this respect has not been obtained. Nevertheless, I hope that within its limitations, the commentary (the first on *Nero*) will be of some use to students of the Julio-Claudian principate. The short bibliography lists the books and articles referred to in the introduction and notes; I have restricted these to recent works in the English language which are of immediate use in amplifying points made in the notes. I have not referred to articles in the standard handbooks except in a very few cases.

All dates are AD unless otherwise indicated, though in some cases where ambiguity might arise, the AD dates have been so specified. References to other *Lives* by Suetonius are by title without the author's name, and references to *Nero* by chapter and section numbers alone.

B.H. Warmington
University of Bristol

Introduction

More is known about C. Suetonius Tranquillus than about most other Latin writers, though even so it is little enough. He is generally supposed to have been born about 70, or perhaps a few years earlier, though the evidence is not strong. His grandfather appears to have been familiar with the court of the emperor Caligula, perhaps as a freedman but more likely as a praetorian guard. His father was Suetonius Laetus – the *cognomina* of the two presumably have some private family significance – who served as an equestrian tribune with the *Legio XIII* on the side of the emperor Otho at the battle of Bedriacum in the civil war of 69 (*Otho* 10). Although Laetus was on the losing side, it seems clear he was not one of those victimised by Vitellius. From a fragmentary inscription discovered at Hippo Regius (Bone) in Algeria and set up in honour of Suetonius Tranquillus, it has been thought that the family had some connection with the place as settlers or landowners; see Townend (1961). It was during the lifetimes of both Laetus and Tranquillus that the North African provinces began to produce men who had equestrian and then senatorial rank. However, it is certain that Suetonius spent most of his life at Rome, and no convincing trace of provincial origin can be detected in his work. He was educated at Rome – his teachers are not known – and was an eyewitness, as a young man, of events towards the end of the reign of Domitian (*Domitian* 12, *Nero* 57). After the death of Domitian in 96, we find him in close contact with Pliny the Younger, his senior by ten years, a man of senatorial rank, soon to be consul in 100, and active as a patron of men of literary talent, among whom Suetonius was to be numbered. At first Suetonius seems to have thought of a career as an advocate but shortly after 96 Pliny wrote to a friend about a piece of property which Suetonius, described as a house-friend, wanted to buy, asking him to see that the vendor put a fair price on it. According to Pliny, Suetonius wanted it because it was close to Rome and a road, was a house of modest size and had sufficient but not too much land for him to enjoy as a scholar (*scholasticus*). Suetonius was therefore already engaged in literary pursuits, which, as his own career was to show, were regarded as a suitable background for office holding. He was presumably wealthy enough to be enrolled among the *equites* and thus eligible for offices of equestrian standing. About 101, Pliny obtained a military tribunate for him through the influence of another senator, but before the appointment was confirmed, Suetonius asked for it to be transferred to a relative, a request to which Pliny agreed. This is a good example of the way patronage worked in imperial Rome, and although we may suppose (perhaps wrongly) that Pliny's characteristic good nature was taxed by Suetonius' change of mind, their friendship continued unbroken. About 105, Pliny wrote to him saying that his delay in publishing his work – no details are given – was disappointing their mutual friends. Later, in 111, he appears to have been on Pliny's staff when the latter was governor of Bithynia; Pliny wrote to the emperor Trajan asking for the important privilege of the *ius trium liberorum* for Suetonius (who was childless), commending him as *virum probissimum honestissimum eruditissimum*. This gave financial and, if he entered public life, career advantages to Suetonius. Again we see the working of patronage and the standing a man of learning could acquire.

It was probably shortly after this that Suetonius did in fact enter on an official career, rather late in the day. The inscription from Hippo appears to say that Trajan made him a member of the panel of *equites* who sat on the juries at Rome. Other minor posts may have followed – the inscription is fragmentary – and he then became in succession *a studiis* and *a bibliothecis*. The duties of the former post are not exactly known but seem to have involved work on the drafting of imperial pronouncements, and advising the emperor about his contacts with the literary world. The post *a bibliothecis* had the supervision of the public libraries at Rome, which by this date were extensive, and also further involvement in the working of imperial patronage of liberal studies. Both posts seem to accord with an easily formed image of Suetonius as a scholar. Finally he became *ab epistulis* to Hadrian shortly after he became emperor in 117. During the first century the post of *ab epistulis* or chief secretary of the emperor had become important as the flow of imperial correspondence increased, and the *ab epistulis* wrote, or at least drafted, imperial replies to petitioners of all sorts, besides overseeing imperial correspondence with provincial governors. Originally an appointment in the emperor's household, under Claudius it was held by Narcissus, the most powerful of his freedmen. Later in the century, Greek literary figures of free birth and equestrian status came to be used for the emperor's Greek correspondence, and during the period from Domitian to Hadrian men of similar status replaced freedmen in the handling of material in Latin, Suetonius being one of the earliest known. Expertise in law or finance was not required, and the development testifies to the importance of literary culture and to Suetonius' own standing in it; see Millar (1977) 90 ff. He may have owed his final promotion to the praetorian prefect Septicius Clarus who had also been a close friend of Pliny (who was now dead) and had been the recipient of the dedication of Pliny's collected letters. But in 121 or 122 they both, together with others, fell from office perhaps during Hadrian's visit to Britain; excessive familiarity with the empress Sabina is alleged by late and unsatisfactory sources (Joh. Lydus, *de Mag.* 2.6; *Hist. Aug., Hadr.* 11.31).

Assuming that the chronology set out here is roughly correct [see Baldwin (1983) 8 ff. for some controversial alternatives], Suetonius was dismissed when little over fifty. Nothing is known of the rest of his life but he appears to have been still alive in 130. We have the titles of many of his works but not their dates except in the case of the *Caesares* (to give a short title to the *de vita Caesarum*), which were probably begun when he was *ab epistulis* and finished when he was out of office. It is clear from Pliny that he must have produced many titles, however brief, before this, if only to warrant continual patronage. The Byzantine compilation known as the *Suda* regarded Suetonius not as an administrator but as a *philologos*, a scholar, and gave a formidable list of his works in both Greek and Latin. Among these were books on Greek games, on words of abuse (both in Greek), on famous courtesans, on Cicero's *de Republica*, on kings, both Roman and non-Roman, on the origins of Roman public offices and on Roman games (*ludicra historia* as it was called). All are lost, but from the material on games and spectacles under most emperors in the *Caesares* it is clear he was using his own collection. Some fragments remain of his *de viris illustribus*, very short lives of literary figures of various sorts such as teachers of rhetoric, historians and poets. Although admired later and used as a model by St. Jerome, these literary lives are hardly to be compared in length and detail with the *Caesares*. It should however be said that to find information about the lives of these persons, who were normally not public figures, was extremely difficult. Although the variety of subjects handled by Suetonius suggests that he was no more than a cultivated dilettante, the same superficial judgement could be made of some of the work of Rome's greatest scholar, M. Terentius Varro (116-27 BC). Suetonius in fact stands in the tradition of Varro in his many-sided interests, though he was probably less assiduous, and he was also a less voluminous writer than either Varro or the encyclopaedist Pliny the Elder (23-79), the uncle of his patron, and also an administrator of equestian rank.

The full title of Suetonius' work on the emperors was *de vita Caesarum*. It was not originally organised as 12 *Lives* (Julius Caesar to Domitian) but in eight books. One book was allotted to each ruler from Julius Caesar to Nero, making six; a seventh covered the short-lived rulers of 68/69 (Galba, Otho and Vitellius), and the eighth dealt with the Flavian emperors. The text is complete with the exception of the dedication to Septicius Clarus and the first few sections of *Divus Julius*. It is possible that the books were not all given to the public together and that the earlier lives were written, or at any rate had preliminary work done on them, while Suetonius was *ab epistulis*; see Townend (1959). A well known feature of the work is that the *Lives* show a consistent decline in quality. *Divus Julius* stands somewhat apart, though it has substantal merits while ignoring what Cicero and Livy had to say. *Divus Augustus* is unique in its wealth of detail, which is not matched in his work on the later Julio-Claudian rulers, of which *Nero* was the last; the remaining *Lives*, even those of the Flavians under whom he spent his youth, are even more insubstantial. The reason for the decline, especially after the death of Nero, can only be surmised. There was little to say of Galba, Otho and Vitellius, whose brief periods of rule were largely taken up with civil war, about which Suetonius was not concerned to write (see below). He may have felt the Flavians, especially Domitian, rather too close for comfort, though Tacitus did not. Perhaps he just lost interest; for his contemporary Juvenal, the reign of Nero seemed already to close an admittedly shameful but an exciting and exotic era.

In some respects biography was the literary form least developed in antiquity. No ancient biographer could approach his subject with the knowledge of psychology available today, and the notion of putting him in the political, economic and social context of his age was lacking. Among the great majority of Greek and Roman biographers, as far as we can tell, since relatively little has survived, the genre always had a pronounced ethical concern and tended to serve didactic purposes. This was evident in the work of Suetonius' great contemporary, Plutarch of Chaeronea (c.50-120), who, as Grant [(1970) 118] put it 'was a convinced adherent of the venerable tradition that the past must be studied so that we may derive some moral uplift in contemplating it'. Suetonius is different in that the amount of moralising is negligible, though this is not to say that he lacked a firm moral standpoint, and there is no evidence of a didactic concern. It is of course true that if we had the dedication and preface we might find that he expressed conventional commonplaces about the value of his work. However, just like biographers with a more definite purpose, he concentrated on the actions and character of his subjects. In excluding what he considered irrelevant he may have adhered more rigidly than most to what has been called the 'Law of Biographical Relevance' (see Townend [1967] 84) but he did not differ in principle in this respect from his Greek predecessors, who tended to include less detail but more explanatory philosophising. The concentration on the actions of the subjects affected the dimensions of Suetonius' *Lives* more than those of most Greek parallels; all are of negligible length compared with modern biographies, yet Suetonius' *Caesares* are many times longer than, for example, the jejune summaries of Cornelius Nepos (99-24 BC). Above all, biography differed from historiography, which for Greek and Roman alike meant narrative history with a pronounced emphasis on military and political history chronologically arranged. Suetonius had so little concern with military history that, for example, he could summarise the wars of Julius Caesar in a few lines.

Although both Greek and Roman literary culture regarded historiography as qualitatively superior to biography, the prestige of the latter had been growing in the first century, the genre being flexible enough to include Tacitus' *Agricola*, the lost lives of victims of Nero by Fannius, and Suetonius' own literary lives. Suetonius was the first Latin writer to attempt to write the lives of Roman emperors although, only shortly before him, Plutarch had written lives of Galba and Otho. What prompted him to adopt the biographical form, other than his habit of using a compilatory method in previous work, is uncertain. He may have felt that Tacitus' historical work, which had recently appeared, could not be emulated; perhaps he believed that biography was more appropriate than the traditional annalistic form to Roman imperial history because it corresponded to historical reality. Even Tacitus, though formally adhering strictly to the annalistic form, could not avoid the natural breaks caused by the deaths and accessions of emperors.

One of the most obvious features of the *Caesares*, the arrangement of the material under separate headings (*per species*) is found in Greek biography as early as Xenophon in the fourth century BC, but Suetonius' choice of the topics he considered essential for inclusion in a life, and his general approach, were thoroughly Roman. Each of the *Lives* contains all or most of the following: family origin, remote ancestors and parents of the subject, the place of his birth, with appropriate omens of his future character, childhood, entry into the public view, accession to the principate, aspects of government including legislation, behaviour in a judicial capacity, public works undertaken and games provided, campaigns (without detail) and various aspects of private and public behaviour. Concern with facts of this sort had long been the basis of the traditional form of *laudationes* – often but not necessarily funeral orations – on great men, and many of the same features can be observed in a work very different from a Suetonian biography, namely Pliny the Younger's panegyric on Trajan, and, in yet another different form, in the semi-autobiographical *Res Gestae* of Augustus himself. Similarly, Suetonius had a traditionally Roman view of what virtues and vices were, and this is exceptionally clear in *Nero*; the values may be simplistic compared with some Greek moral philosophy, or even Cicero and Seneca, but they are firmly rooted in the social outlook of the Roman tradition. Furthermore, although the great majority of Suetonius' possible models, whether biographies or *laudationes*, were of approved characters and hence concentrated on the virtues, he had no difficulty in writing five major *Lives* (*Tiberius, Caligula, Claudius, Nero* and *Domitian*) which were not just critical but almost totally hostile. These emperors had been condemned outright by the social class to which he belonged and in the historical sources he used. Here too, however, there was a long standing Roman tradition. The malevolent treatment of Catiline by Sallust shows how personalities could be denigrated and Cicero's *Verrine Orations* are also relevant. The indiscriminate allegations of all sorts of depravity, with details, however unfounded, had been traditional in the political and judicial contests of the republican era and provided the language and rhetoric used to discredit emperors – once they were safely dead. Even Tacitus, who expressed his own misgivings about the reliability of such posthumous abuse, nevertheless reproduced much of it with little hesitation.

The lack of chronological detail for which Suetonius is often criticised is in fact common to all ancient biographers. In any case, the brevity which was customary for the genre in which he was writing, as well as elementary concern for style, made it impossible for him to keep referring to consular years, a highly inconvenient method of dating, or to give more than the occasional reference to the age of his subject. In the case of *Nero* it can be shown that within the general arrangement *per species* the details are normally listed in chronological order though not, unfortunately for the historian, with complete consistency. Suetonius' conception of character, like that of most ancient writers, was essentially static; a man was born with a certain disposition which manifested itself during his life as and when age, opportunity and the lack of external restraints allowed. Thus, although Tacitus covered Nero's principate annalistically, he did not provide much more sense of character development than Suetonius. A more serious defect in the biographer was his failure in all the *Lives* to relate the actions of his subjects to developing political situations or even to changes in Roman society; this was implicit in his arrangement of material under the various headings. Nero's cultural pretensions and his wholehearted enthusiasm for Greek culture are only described anecdotally, and their significance for Rome remains unexamined, in spite of the fact that there was an ebb and flow in the process of Roman acculturation to Hellenistic influences. It is also surprisingly difficult to show that his experience at the heart of the imperial government as *ab epistulis* to Hadrian had any effect on what he had to say about the earlier emperors.

Suetonius' style reflects his rejection of the explicit moralising, highly coloured descriptive writing, and dramatic presentation of crises which were a feature of Roman historiography in such diverse writers as Sallust, Livy and Tacitus. He avoids almost all traditional rhetorical devices. There is little elaboration of subordinate clauses, nor does he seek to express himself sententiously. There seems to be a deliberate attempt to fit the language to the listing of factual details, and in many cases the sentence structure is closely connected with the content. This is not to say that his style is clear and straightforward like that of Caesar (whose force and clarity in any case had their own part in his self-justification); it avoids the prolixity of Pliny the Elder but can be unduly compressed in an attempt to include as much material as possible with the brevity of his chosen form. Only isolated episodes, such as the last days of Nero, reveal a talent for concentrated and dramatic presentation of events.

Suetonius can and no doubt should be read as the best exemplar of a specific form, Latin biography, far removed from our concepts of the biographical genre. But the historian is bound to want more, and to ask at almost every line (of *Nero*) – is it true? The question of the reliability of *Nero* is bound up with the question of the sources used by Suetonius, the extent of unwritten collective memory being unknowable. Like nearly all ancient biographical writers – and historians as well for that matter – he used written historical accounts by earlier writers as the basis of his work. Also available were the lost memoirs of Nero's mother, Agrippina, whatever they may have contained, and the descriptions of the deaths of distinguished victims of Nero by Fannius. Some of his own researches on Roman games and spectacles, a significant feature under Nero, were naturally used. There seem to have been many witticisms of Nero apart from those known in other sources besides Suetonius which he found in sources unknown to us. In the earlier *Lives* he had quoted verbatim from letters of Augustus, a major stroke of originality out of line with the universal practice of writers up to his time, but these were only used to illustrate matters of a private nature in the imperial family. For whatever reason, such documents were no longer available to him when he wrote on Nero.

It seems possible that he wrote under the assumption that his readership knew the outlines of the general course of events in the early principate sufficiently well for him to compress, or even exclude, a huge amount of material one would have supposed essential to a full appreciation of what he was writing. This (in itself an assumption) would indicate a readership interested in works of history in the traditional form, and such were certainly available. The many similarities between Suetonius, Tacitus and the later Greek writer, Dio Cassius, in their accounts of Nero are all the more striking in view of the different forms in which the two Latin authors were writing and the heavily rhetorical production of Dio, even in the excerpted form in which we have his work. It is not just a question of Nero being viewed as a disaster for Rome, but of many identical details. The notes to the text in this edition indicate where these are described by the three authors in similar ways and with verbal coincidences so pronounced as to leave no doubt they were using at least one common source. It does admittedly seem certain that Suetonius knew of the work of Tacitus but did not make direct use of him.

That all three used a common source has been recognised for a century or more and it may be presumed that in spite of all the analytical work done on the problem, certainty as to the identity of the lost historian will never be reached. The view taken here is that the chief source of the three writers was probably the (lost) historical work of Pliny the Elder. This author's *Natural History*, published in 77, reveals that he had already written a historical work but that it would not be published until after his death, which took place when he fell victim to the eruption of Vesuvius in 79. The lost work in 31 books seems to have covered the years 41-71 and was certainly used by Tacitus who refers to it twice. A number of hostile references to Nero occur even in the *Natural History*, some of them verbally identical with passages in one or more of the three later writers; it is assumed that Pliny copied these from his unpublished history. The nature of his historical work is variously estimated; from his surviving work we may deduce that he was verbose, uncritical in assembling material, and quite prepared to retail sensational anecdotes and exaggerated criticism of historical persons, including Nero. Far less is known of two other historians, Cluvius Rufus (see note on 21.2 below) and Fabius Rusticus, both quoted by Tacitus as historians of the principate of Nero, but it is logically possible that one or both provided material used by more than one of our three surviving accounts. On this subject, see Warmington (1969) 1-9, and for a different view Syme (1958) 287-303. Thus, if the character of Pliny's work was as described, much of the sensational material, true or false, had been written up within a decade of the death of Nero; Cluvius Rufus also seems to have written under Vespasian.

Inevitably, Tacitus has always been and will remain our primary source for Nero's principate. Apart from anything else, he includes substantial accounts of events in Britain and Armenia which Suetonius ignores. Yet his highly mannered and idiosyncratic approach should not allow us to forget the basic truth, shown by comparison with Suetonius and Dio, that the identical information which they transmit from their source or sources is not simply about items of major importance but also about rumour and anecdote. There are few stories to the discredit of Nero which are not to be found in Tacitus as well as the others. It is true that Tacitus is somewhat more cautious than Suetonius who is more likely to accept as truth what Tacitus has doubts about; an obvious case is the allegation that Nero set fire to Rome. Yet it is surprising how frequently Suetonius hedges by attributing some anecdote to rumour or common report (e.g. 7.1; 23.2; 28.2; 29; 30.3; 32.3; 34.3; 36.2). Perhaps the fact that the phenomenon is not frequently remarked upon, except to condemn Suetonius for evasion or unwillingness to make up his mind, is significant; both criticisms may be justified, but it is also arguable that so overwhelming is the cumulative effect of the discreditable anecdotes that the reader forgets the disclaimers, and indeed is meant to do so. Only the more attentive will notice similar caution when it occurs in Tacitus, whose narrative almost always emphasises the more damaging allegations. Since we have no external control for judging the truth of the stories, though some are so outrageous that Suetonius' inclusion of them can hardly be condoned (e.g. 37.2, not mentioned by any other source), it might be said that if Suetonius is condemned for his uncritical transmission of dubious material, similar condemnation must fall on Tacitus, who is superficially more fastidious. Just as reprehensible from the point of view of the historian is his habit of generalising from a particular instance of which details were certainly available to him. It is also worth remarking on what he omitted, in addition to military matters. There is not a word on the praetorian prefect Tigellinus, so important in Tacitus' account, and hardly a word on Seneca, the Pisonian conspiracy, or the Stoic and literary victims of Nero. This may have been deliberate, since it is known Suetonius was out of sympathy with both Lucan and Seneca as literary figures.

Attempts have been made from time to time to rehabilitate Nero by rejecting all the discreditable material as mere defamatory fiction emanating from a bitterly hostile upper class, alienated by his philhellenism, showmanship and popularity with the proletariat in the city of Rome, and by attributing to Nero vast schemes of a beneficial character on the strength of a few favourable indications, a number actually from Suetonius; his listing of actions by Nero which he viewed favourably is unique. No doubt the anti-Neronian stories lost nothing in the telling, and it is true that our surviving accounts all stem from the social milieu most offended by Nero. But there is little evidence that the general government of the empire under Nero was any better, though it may well have been no worse, than it was under other emperors. He won a better reputation in the Greek world, which was obviously flattered by his philhellenism and the grant of freedom to the province of Achaea; but projects which might have brought some benefit to Rome and Italy would have been paid for by provincial tributes. There were strong social forces at work in Italy leading towards a century of somewhat more stable and effective administration of the empire than that provided by the last of the Julio-Claudians.

There is no doubt that Suetonius' biographical approach was the one which appealed to later generations, though the virtual disappearance of Latin historiography for several centuries is easier to assert than explain. In the third century Marius Maximus wrote imperial biographies, and in the fourth the author of the *Historia Augusta* what passed as such, and even the slender summaries of Aurelius Victor and Eutropius stem ultimately from Suetonius. No doubt the form met such needs as were felt for knowledge of recent times better than history written in the traditional manner; see Townend (1967) 108. In any case it was the history of the republican age, or at least its almost legendary heroes, which took pride of place in what educated Romans learned of the past. In the second century Suetonius' relatively simple and unselfconscious style was perhaps appreciated when the highly mannered writing of Tacitus went out of fashion and, while his readership would have agreed with his traditional standpoint on what was to be expected from an emperor, it might also have felt that explicit moralising was better left to imperial panegyrics, in which the emperor's virtues and the vices of his enemies could be dealt with in a highly rhetorical manner. Lastly, it was not so much the mixture of rumour, scandal and scurrility but the artful blending of information with vivid anecdote within a very few pages that made Suetonius one of the most widely read of classical authors from the time of the Renaissance.

Structure of *Nero*

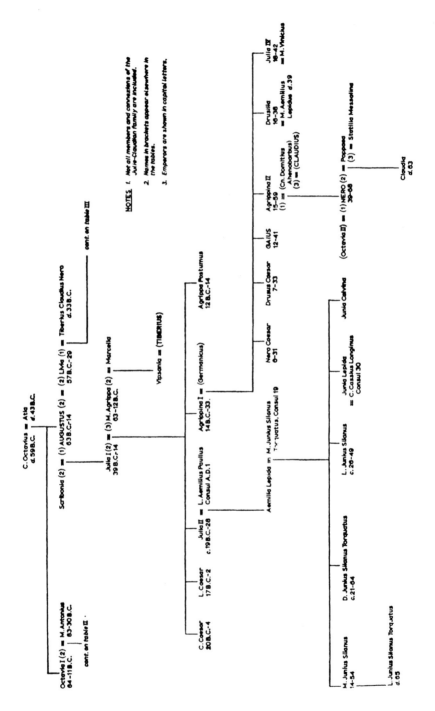

C. Octavius = Atia
d.59B.C.

Octavia I (2) = M. Antonius
64–11B.C. 83–30 B.C.

cont. on table II

Scribonia (2) = (1) AUGUSTUS (2) = (2) Livia (1) = Tiberius Claudius Nero
                63B.C.–14   57B.C.–29   d.33B.C.

cont. on table III

Julia I (2) = (3) M. Agrippa (2) = Marcella
39B.C.–14   63–12B.C.

Vipsania = (TIBERIUS)

C. Caesar   L. Caesar   Julia II   Agrippina I   Agrippa Postumus
20B.C.–4   17B.C.–2   c.19B.C.–28   14B.C.–33.   12 B.C.–14
                                  = L. Aemilius Paullus = (Germanicus)
                                    Consul A.D.1

Aemilia Lepida = M. Junius Silanus
                 Torquatus, Consul 19

Nero Caesar   Drusus Caesar   GAIUS   Agrippina II
6–31   7–33   12–41   15–59
                                                (1) = (Cn. Domitius
                                                       Ahenobarbus)
                                                (3) = (CLAUDIUS)

D. Junius Silanus Torquatus   L. Junius Silanus   Junia Lepida   Junia Calvina   (Octavia II) = (1) NERO (2) = Poppaea
c.21–64   c.26–49   = C. Cassius Longinus   39–68   (3) = Statilia Messalina
                                                      Consul 30

M. Junius Silanus
14–54

L. Junius Silanus Torquatus
d. 65

                                                                          Claudia
                                                                          d.63

Drusilla   Julia IV
16–38   18–42
= M. Aemilius = M. Vinicius
  Lepidus d.39

NOTES 1. Not all members and connexions of the
Julio-Claudian family are included.

2. Names in brackets appear elsewhere in
the tables.

3. Emperors are shown in capital letters.

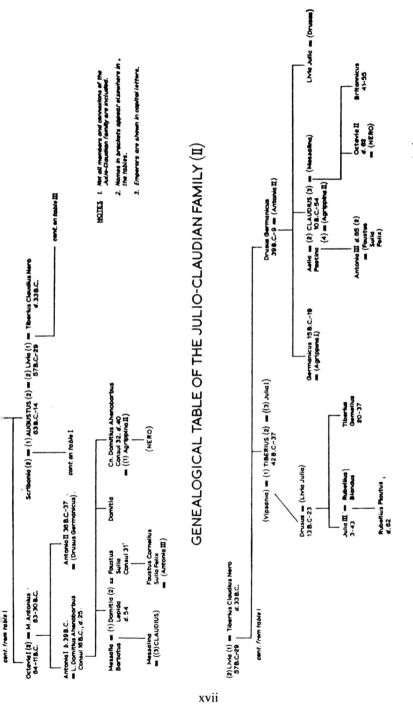

GENEALOGICAL TABLE OF THE JULIO-CLAUDIAN FAMILY (II)

GENEALOGICAL TABLE OF THE JULIO-CLAUDIAN FAMILY (III)

NOTES 1 Not all members and connexions of the Julio-Claudian family are included.

2. Names in brackets appear elsewhere in the tables.

3. Emperors are shown in capital letters.

xvii

Essential Dates

Main Events of Nero's Life and Principate

Birth of Nero	37
Adoption by Claudius	49
Marries Octavia	53
Becomes emperor	54
Beginning of Armenian war	54
Murder of Agrippina	59
Revolt of Boudicca in Britain	60
Death of Burrus and retirement of Seneca	62
Execution of Octavia and Nero's marriage to Poppaea	64
Fire of Rome	65
Conspiracy of Piso	66
Visit of Tiridates to Rome	66
Nero's tour of Greece	68
Revolt of Vindex and Galba and fall of Nero	68

Roman Emperors from Augustus to Hadrian

Augustus	31 BC-14
Tiberius	14 BC-37 AD
Gaius (Caligula)	37-41
Claudius	41-54
Nero	54-68
Galba	68-69
Otho	69
Vitellius	69
Vespasian	69-79
Titus	79-81
Domitian	81-96
Nerva	96-98
Trajan	98-117
Hadrian	117-138

Bibliography

Baldwin, B., *Suetonius* (Amsterdam, 1983).

Balsdon, J.P.V.D., *Life and Leisure in Ancient Rome* (London, 1969).

Bradley, K.R., *Suetonius Nero: A Historical Commentary* (Collection Latomus 157, Brussels, 1978).

Boethius, A., *The Golden House of Nero* (Michigan, 1961).

Brunt, P.A., 'The Revolt of Vindex', *Latomus* 18 (1959) 531 ff.

Cameron, A.D.E., *Circus Factions* (Oxford, 1976).

Charlesworth, M.P., 'Nero; Some Aspects', *Journal of Roman Studies* 40 (1950) 69 ff.

Chilver, G.F., 'The Army in Politics', *Journal of Roman Studies* 47 (1957) 29 ff.

Dudley, D.R., *Urbs Roma* (London, 1967).

Gallivan, P.A., 'The False Neros: a Reconsideration', *Historia* 22 (1973) 364 f.

——'Suetonius and Chronology in the de vita Neronis', *Historia* 23 (1974) 297 ff.

——'Confusion concerning the age of Octavia', *Latomus* 33 (1974) 116 f.

Grant, M., *The Ancient Historians* (London, 1970).

Griffin, M.T., *Seneca; a Philosopher in Politics* (Oxford, 1976).

——*Nero: The End of a Dynasty* (London, 1984).

Hainsworth, J.H., 'Verginius and Vindex', *Historia* 11 (1962) 86 ff.

Magie, D., *Roman Rule in Asia Minor* (Princeton, 1950).

Millar, F., 'The *Aerarium* and its Officials under the Empire', *Journal of Roman Studies* 54 (1964) 33 ff.

——*The Emperor in the Roman World* (London, 1977).

Rogers, R.S., 'The Neronian Comets', *Transactions of the American Philological Association* 84 (1953) 240 ff.

Sandford, E.M., 'Nero and the East', *Harvard Studies in Classical Philology* 48 (1937) 75 ff.

Smallwood, E.M., *Documents illustrating the Principates of Gaius, Claudius and Nero* (Cambridge, 1967).

Syme, R., *The Roman Revolution* (Oxford, 1939).

——*Tacitus* (Oxford, 1958).

Townend, G.,'The Date of Composition of Suetonius' *Caesares*', *Classical Quarterly* 9 (1959) 285 ff.

——'The Hippo Inscription and the Career of Suetonius', *Historia* 10 (1961) 99 ff.

——'Suetonius and his Influence', in T.A. Dorey (ed.): *Latin Biography* (London, 1969).

Wallace-Hadrill, A., *Suetonius* (London, 1983).

Warmington, B.H., *Nero, Reality and Legend* (London, 1969).

——'Nero, Boudicca and the Frontier in the West', in K. Branigan and P.J. Fowler (eds): *The Roman West Country* (Newton Abbott, 1976).

Abbreviations

AE:	L'Année Epigraphique.
BMC:	British Museum Catalogue of Coins of the Roman Empire.
CIL:	*Corpus Inscriptionum Latinarum.*
ILS:	*Inscriptiones Latinae Selectace*, (ed.) H. Dessau.
PIR:	*Prosopographia Imperii Romani*, 2nd edn, E. Groag and A. Stein.
PW:	Real-Encyclopädie der Klassischen Altertumswissenschaft, eds A. Pauly, G. Wissowa and W. Kroll.

C. Suetoni Tranquilli: De Vita Caesarum

Liber VI: Nero

1.1 Ex gente Domitia duae familiae claruerunt, Calvinorum et Ahenobarborum. Ahenobarbi auctorem originis itemque cognominis habent L. Domitium, cui rure quondam revertenti iuvenes gemini augustiore forma ex occursu imperasse traduntur, nuntiaret senatui ac populo victoriam, de qua incertum adhuc erat; atque in fidem maiestatis adeo permulsisse malas, ut e nigro rutilum aerique adsimilem capillum redderent. quod insigne mansit et in posteris eius, ac magna pars rutila barba fuerunt. **1.2** functi autem consulatibus septem, triumpho censuraque duplici et inter patricios adlecti perseveraverunt omnes in eodem cognomine ac ne praenomina quidem ulla praeterquam Gnaei et Luci usurparunt; eaque ipsa notabili varietate, modo continuantes unum quodque per trinas personas, modo alternantes per singulas. nam primum secundumque ac tertium Ahenobarborum Lucios, sequentis rursus tres ex ordine Gnaeos accepimus, reliquos non nisi vicissim tum Lucios tum Gnaeos. pluris e familia cognosci referre arbitror, quo facilius appareat ita degenerasse a suorum virtutibus Nero, ut tamen vitia cuiusque quasi tradita et ingenita rettulerit.

2.1 ut igitur paulo altius repetam, atavus eius Cn. Domitius in tribunatu pontificibus offensior, quod alium quam se in patris sui locum cooptassent, ius sacerdotum subrogandorum a collegiis ad populum transtulit; at in consulatu Allobrogibus Arvernisque superatis elephanto per provinciam vectus est turba militum quasi inter sollemnia triumphi prosequente. **2.2** in hunc dixit Licinius Crassus orator non esse mirandum, quod aeneam barbam haberet, cui os ferreum, cor plumbeum esset. huius filius praetor C. Caesarem abeuntem consulatu, quem adversus auspicia legesque gessisse existimabatur, ad disquisitionem senatus vocavit; mox consul imperatorem ab exercitibus Gallicis retrahere temptavit successorque ei per factionem nominatus principio civilis belli ad Corfinium captus est. **2.3** unde dimissus Massiliensis obsidione laborantis cum adventu suo confirmasset, repente destituit acieque demum Pharsalica occubuit; vir neque satis constans et ingenio truci in desperatione rerum mortem timore appetitam ita expavit, ut haustum venenum paenitentia evomuerit medicumque manumiserit, quod sibi prudens ac sciens minus noxium temperasset. consultante autem Cn. Pompeio de mediis ac neutram partem sequentibus solus censuit hostium numero habendos.

3.1 reliquit filium omnibus gentis suae procul dubio praeferendum. is inter conscios Caesarianae necis quamquam insons damnatus lege Pedia, cum ad Cassium Brutumque se propinqua sibi cognatione iunctos contulisset, post utriusque interitum classem olim commissam retinuit, auxit etiam, nec nisi partibus ubique profligatis M. Antonio sponte et ingentis meriti loco tradidit. **3.**2 solusque omnium ex iis, qui pari lege damnati erant, restitutus in patriam amplissimos honores percucurrit; ac subinde redintegrata dissensione civili, eidem Antonio legatus, delatam sibi summam imperii ab iis, quos Cleopatrae pudebat, neque suscipere neque recusare fidenter propter subitam valitudinem ausus, transiit ad Augustum et in diebus paucis obiit, nonnulla et ipse infamia aspersus. nam Antonius eum desiderio amicae Serviliae Naidis transfugisse iactavit.

4.1 ex hoc Domitius nascitur, quem emptorem familiae pecuniaeque in testamento Augusti fuisse mox vulgo notatum est, non minus aurigandi arte in adulescentia clarus quam deinde ornamentis triumphalibus ex Germanico bello. verum arrogans, profusus, immitis censorem L. Plancum via sibi decedere aedilis coegit; praeturae consulatusque honore equites R. matronasque ad agendum mimum produxit in scaenam. venationes et in circo et in omnibus urbis regionibus dedit, munus etiam gladiatorium, sed tanta saevitia, ut necesse fuerit Augusto clam frustra monitum edicto coercere.

5.1 ex Antonia maiore patrem Neronis procreavit omni parte vitae detestabilem, siquidem comes ad Orientem C. Caesaris iuvenis, occiso liberto suo, quod potare quantum iubebatur recusarat, dimissus e cohorte amicorum nihilo modestius vixit; sed et in viae Appiae vico repente puerum citatis iumentis haud ignarus obtrivit et Romae medio foro cuidam equiti R. liberius iurganti oculum eruit; **5.2** perfidiae vero tantae, ut non modo argentarios pretiis rerum coemptarum, sed et in praetura mercede palmarum aurigarios fraudaverit, notatus ob haec et sororis ioco....querentibus dominis factionum repraesentanda praemia in posterum sanxit. maiestatis quoque et adulteriorum incestique cum sorore Lepida sub excessu Tiberi reus, mutatione temporum evasit decessitque Pyrgis morbo aquae intercutis, sublato filio Nerone ex Agrippina Germanico genita.

6.1 Nero natus est Anti post IX mensem quam Tiberius excessit, XVIII. Kal. Ian. tantum quod exoriente sole, paene ut radiis prius quam terra contingeretur. de genitura eius statim multa et formidulosa multis coniectantibus praesagio fuit etiam Domiti patris vox, inter gratulationes amicorum negantis quicquam ex se et Agrippina nisi detestabile et malo publico nasci potuisse. **6.2** eiusdem futurae infelicitatis signum evidens die lustrico exstitit; nam C. Caesar, rogante sorore ut infanti quod vellet nomen daret, intuens Claudium patruum suum, a quo mox principe Nero adoptatus est, eius se dixit dare, neque ipse serio sed per iocum et aspernante Agrippina, quod tum Claudius inter ludibria aulae erat. **6.3** trimulus patrem amisit; cuius ex parte tertia heres, ne hanc quidem integram cepit correptis per coheredem Gaium universis bonis. et subinde matre etiam relegata paene inops atque egens apud amitam Lepidam nutritus est sub duobus paedagogis saltatore atque tonsore. verum Claudio imperium adepto non solum paternas opes reciperavit, sed et Crispi Passieni vitrici sui hereditate ditatus est. **6.**4 gratia quidem et potentia revocatae restitutaeque matris usque eo floruit, ut emanaret in vulgus missos a Messalina uxore Claudi, qui eum meridiantem, quasi Britannici aemulum, strangularent. additum fabulae eosdem dracone e pulvino se proferente conterritos refugisse. quae fabula exorta est deprensis in lecto eius circum cervicalia serpentis exuviis; quas tamen aureae armillae ex voluntate matris inclusas dextro brachio gestavit aliquamdiu ac taedio tandem maternae memoriae abiecit rursusque extremis suis rebus frustra requisiit.

7.1 tener adhuc necdum matura pueritia circensibus ludis Troiam constantissime favorabiliterque lusit. undecimo aetatis anno a Claudio adoptatus est Annaeoque Senecae iam tunc senatori in disciplinam traditus. ferunt Senecam proxima nocte visum sibi per quietem C. Caesari praecipere, et fidem somnio Nero brevi fecit prodita immanitate naturae quibus primum potuit experimentis. namque Britannicum fratrem, quod se post adoptionem Ahenobarbum ex consuetudine salutasset, ut subditivum apud patrem arguere conatus est. amitam autem Lepidam ream testimonio coram afflixit gratificans matri, a qua rea premebatur. **7.**2 deductus in forum tiro populo congiarium, militi donativum proposuit indictaque decursione praetorianis scutum sua manu praetulit; exin patri gratias in senatu egit. apud eundem consulem pro Bononiensibus Latine, pro Rhodiis atque Iliensibus Graece verba fecit. auspicatus est et iuris dictionem praefectus urbi sacro Latinarum, celeberrimis patronis non tralaticias, ut assolet, et brevis, sed maximas plurimasque postulationes certatim ingerentibus, quamvis interdictum a Claudio esset. nec multo post duxit uxorem Octaviam ediditque pro Claudi salute circenses et venationem.

8.1 septemdecim natus annos, ut de Claudio palam factum est, inter horam sextam septimamque processit ad excubitores, cum ob totius diei diritatem non aliud auspicandi tempus accommodatius videretur; proque Palati gradibus imperator consalutatus lectica in castra et inde raptim appellatis militibus in curiam delatus est discessitque iam vesperi, ex immensis, quibus cumulabatur, honoribus tantum patris patriae nomine recusato propter aetatem.

9.1 orsus hinc a pietatis ostentatione Claudium apparatissimo funere elatum laudavit et consecravit. memoriae Domiti patris honores maximos habuit. matri summam omnium rerum privatarum publicarumque permisit. primo etiam imperii die signum excubanti tribuno dedit optimam matrem ac deinceps eiusdem saepe lectica per publicum simul vectus est. Antium coloniam deduxit ascriptis veteranis e praetorio additisque per domicilii translationem ditissimis primipilarium; ubi et portum operis sumptuosissimi fecit.

in order to show his true nature tho more clearly

10.1 atque ut certiorem adhuc indolem ostenderet, ex Augusti praescripto imperaturum se professus, neque liberalitatis neque clementiae, ne comitatis quidem exhibendae ullam occasionem omisit. graviora vectigalia aut abolevit aut minuit. praemia delatorum Papiae legis ad quartas redegit. divisis populo viritim quadringenis nummis senatorum nobilissimo cuique, sed a re familiari destituto annua salaria et quibusdam quingena constituit, item praetorianis cohortibus frumentum menstruum gratuitum. **10.2** et cum de supplicio cuiusdam capite damnati ut ex more subscriberet admoneretur: quam vellem, inquit, nescire litteras. omnis ordines subinde ac memoriter salutavit. agenti senatui gratias respondit: cum meruero. ad campestres exercitationes suas admisit et plebem declamavitque saepius publice; recitavit et carmina, non modo domi sed et in theatro, tanta universorum laetitia, ut ob recitationem supplicatio decreta sit eaque pars carminum aureis litteris Iovi Capitolino dicata.

11.1 spectaculorum plurima et varia genera edidit: iuvenales, circenses, scaenicos ludos, gladiatorium munus. iuvenalibus senes quoque consulares anusque matronas recepit ad lusum. circensibus loca equiti secreta a ceteris tribuit commisitque etiam camelorum quadrigas. **11.2** ludis, quos pro aeternitate imperii susceptos appellari maximos voluit, ex utroque ordine et sexu plerique ludicras partes sustinuerunt; notissimus eques R. elephanto supersidens per catadromum decucurrit; inducta Afrani togata, quae Incendium inscribitur, concessumque ut scaenici ardentis domus supellectilem diriperent ac sibi haberent; sparsa et populo missilia omnium rerum per omnes dies: singula cotidie milia avium cuiusque generis, multiplex penus, tesserae frumentariae, vestis, aurum, argentum, gemmae, margaritae, tabulae pictae, mancipia, iumenta atque etiam mansuetae ferae, novissime naves, insulae, agri.

12.1 hos ludos spectavit e proscaeni fastigio. munere, quod in amphitheatro ligneo regione Martii campi intra anni spatium fabricato dedit, neminem occidit, ne noxiorum quidem. exhibuit autem ad ferrum etiam quadringentos senatores sescentosque equites Romanos et quosdam fortunae atque existimationis integrae, ex isdem ordinibus confectores quoque ferarum et varia harenae ministeria. exhibuit et naumachiam marina aqua innantibus beluis; item pyrrhichas quasdam e numero epheborum, quibus post editam operam diplomata civitatis Romanae singulis optulit. **12.2** inter pyrrhicharum argumenta taurus Pasiphaam ligneo iuvencae simulacro abditam iniit, ut multi spectantium crediderunt; Icarus primo statim conatu iuxta cubiculum eius decidit ipsumque cruore respersit. nam perraro praesidere, ceterum accubans, parvis primum foraminibus, deinde toto podio adaperto spectare consueverat. **12.3** instituit et quinquennale certamen primus omnium Romae more Graeco triplex, musicum gymnicum equestre, quod appellavit Neronia; dedicatisque thermis atque gymnasio senatui quoque et equiti oleum praebuit. magistros toto certamini praeposuit consulares sorte, sede praetorum.

deinde in orchestram senatumque descendit et orationis quidem carminisque Latini coronam, de qua honestissimus quisque contenderat, ipsorum consensu concessam sibi recepit, citharae autem a iudicibus ad se delatam adoravit ferrique ad Augusti statuam iussit. **12.4** gymnico, quod in Saeptis edebat, inter buthysiae apparatum barbam primam posuit conditamque in auream pyxidem et pretiosissimis margaritis adornatam Capitolio consecravit. ad athletarum spectaculum invitavit et virgines Vestales, quia Olympiae quoque Cereris sacerdotibus spectare conceditur.

13.1 non immerito inter spectacula ab eo edita et Tiridatis in urbem introitum rettulerim. quem Armeniae regem magnis pollicitationibus sollicitatum, cum destinato per edictum die ostensurus populo propter nubilum distulisset, produxit quo opportunissime potuit, dispositis circa fori templa armatis cohortibus, curuli residens apud rostra triumphantis habitu inter signa militaria atque vexilla. **13.2** et primo per devexum pulpitum subeuntem admisit ad genua adlevatumque dextra exosculatus est, dein precanti tiara deducta diadema inposuit, verba supplicis interpretata praetorio viro multitudini pronuntiante; perductum inde in theatrum ac rursus supplicantem iuxta se latere dextro conlocavit. ob quae imperator consalutatus, laurea in Capitolium lata, Ianum geminum clausit, tamquam nullo residuo bello.

14.1 consulatus quattuor gessit: primum bimenstrem, secundum et novissimum semenstres, tertium quadrimenstrem; medios duos continuavit, reliquos inter annua spatia variavit.

15.1 in iuris dictione postulatoribus nisi sequenti die ac per libellos non temere respondit. cognoscendi morem eum tenuit, ut continuis actionibus omissis singillatim quaeque per vices ageret. quotiens autem ad consultandum secederet, neque in commune quicquam neque propalam deliberabat, sed et conscriptas ab uno quoque sententias tacitus ac secreto legens, quod ipsi libuisset perinde atque pluribus idem videretur pronuntiabat. **15.2** in curiam libertinorum filios diu non admisit; admissis a prioribus principibus honores denegavit. candidatos, qui supra numerum essent, in solacium dilationis ac morae legionibus praeposuit. consulatum in senos plerumque menses dedit. defunctoque circa Kal. Ian. altero e consulibus neminem substituit improbans exemplum vetus Canini Rebili uno die consulis. triumphalia ornamenta etiam quaestoriae dignitatis et nonnullis ex equestri ordine tribuit nec utique de causa militari. de quibusdam rebus orationes ad senatum missas praeterito quaestoris officio per consulem plerumque recitabat.

16.1 formam aedificiorum urbis novam excogitavit et ut ante insulas ac domos porticus essent, de quarum solariis incendia arcerentur; easque sumptu suo exstruxit. destinarat etiam Ostia tenus moenia promovere atque inde fossa mare veteri urbi inducere. **16.2** multa sub eo et animadversa severe et coercita nec minus instituta: adhibitus sumptibus modus; publicae cenae ad sportulas redactae; interdictum ne quid in popinis cocti praeter legumina aut holera veniret, cum antea nullum non obsonii genus proponeretur; affecti suppliciis Christiani, genus hominum superstitionis novae ac maleficae; vetiti quadrigariorum lusus, quibus inveterata licentia passim vagantibus fallere ac furari per iocum ius erat; pantomimorum factiones cum ipsis simul relegatae;

17.1 adversus falsarios tunc primum repertum, ne tabulae nisi pertusae ac ter lino per foramina traiecto obsignarentur; cautum ut testamentis primae duae cerae testatorum modo nomine inscripto vacuae signaturis ostenderentur, ac ne qui alieni testamenti scriptor legatum sibi ascriberet; item ut litigatores pro patrociniis certam iustamque mercedem, pro subselliis nullam omnino darent praebente aerario gratuita; utque rerum actu ab aerario causae ad forum ac reciperatores transferrentur et ut omnes appellationes a iudicibus ad senatum fierent.

18.1 augendi propagandique imperii neque voluntate ulla neque spe motus umquam, etiam ex Britannia deducere exercitum cogitavit, nec nisi verecundia, ne obtrectare parentis gloriae videretur, destitit. Ponti modo regnum concedente Polemone, item Alpium defuncto Cottio in provinciae formam redegit.

19.1 peregrinationes duas omnino suscepit, Alexandrinam et Achaicam; sed Alexandrina ipso profectionis die destitit turbatus religione simul ac periculo. nam cum circumitis templis in aede Vestae resedisset, consurgenti ei primum lacinia obhaesit, dein tanta oborta caligo est, ut dispicere non posset. **19.2** in Achaia Isthmum perfodere adgressus praetorianos pro contione ad incohandum opus cohortatus est tubaque signo dato primus rastello humum effodit et corbulae congestam umeris extulit. parabat et ad Caspias portas expeditionem conscripta ex Italicis senum pedum tironibus nova legione, quam Magni Alexandri phalanga appellabat. **19.3** haec partim nulla reprehensione, partim etiam non mediocri laude digna in unum contuli, ut secernerem a probris ac sceleribus eius, de quibus dehinc dicam.

20.1 inter ceteras disciplinas pueritiae tempore imbutus et musica, statim ut imperium adeptus est, Terpnum citharoedum vigentem tunc praeter alios arcessiit diebusque continuis post cenam canenti in multam noctem assidens paulatim et ipse meditari exercerique coepit neque eorum quicquam omittere, quae generis eius artifices vel conservandae vocis causa vel augendae factitarent; sed et plumbeam chartam supinus pectore sustinere et clystere vomituque purgari et abstinere pomis cibisque officientibus; donec blandiente profectu, quamquam exiguae vocis et fuscae, prodire in scaenam concupiit, subinde inter familiares Graecum proverbium iactans occultae musicae nullum esse respectum. **20.2** et prodit Neapoli primum ac ne concusso quidem repente motu terrae theatro ante cantare destitit, quam incohatum absoluerat nomon. ibidem saepius et per complures cantavit dies; sumpto etiam ad reficiendam vocem brevi tempore, impatiens secreti a balineis in theatrum transiit mediaque in orchestra frequente populo epulatus, si paulum subbibisset, aliquid se sufferi tinniturum Graeco sermone promisit. **20.**3 captus autem modulatis Alexandrinorum laudationibus, qui de novo commeatu Neapolim confluxerant, plures Alexandria evocavit. neque eo segnius adulescentulos equestris ordinis et quinque amplius milia e plebe robustissimae iuventutis undique elegit, qui divisi in factiones plausuum genera condiscerent – bombos et imbrices et testas vocabant – operamque navarent cantanti sibi insignes pinguissima coma et excellentissimo cultu puris ac sine anulo laevis, quorum duces quadringena milia sestertia merebant.

21.1 cum magni aestimaret cantare etiam Romae, Neroneum agona ante praestitutam diem revocavit flagitantibusque cunctis caelestem vocem respondit quidem in hortis se copiam volentibus facturum, sed adiuvante vulgi preces etiam statione militum, quae tunc excubabat, repraesentaturum se pollicitus est libens; ac sine mora nomen suum in albo profitentium citharoedorum iussit ascribi sorticulaque in urnam cum ceteris demissa intravit ordine suo, simul praefecti praetorii citharam sustinentes, post tribuni militum iuxtaque amicorum intimi. **21.**2 utque constitit, peracto principio, Niobam se cantaturum per Cluvium Rufum consularem pronuntiavit et in horam fere decimam perseveravit coronamque eam et reliquam certaminis partem in annum sequentem distulit, ut saepius canendi occasio esset. quod cum tardum videretur, non cessavit identidem se publicare. dubitavit etiam an privatis spectaculis operam inter scaenicos daret quodam praetorum sestertium decies offerente. **21.**3 tragoedias quoque cantavit personatus heroum deorumque, item heroidum ac dearum, personis effectis ad similitudinem oris sui et feminae, prout quamque diligeret. inter cetera cantavit Canacen parturientem, Oresten matricidam, Oedipodem excaecatum, Herculem insanum. in qua fabula fama est tirunculum militem positum ad custodiam aditus, cum eum ornari ac vinciri catenis, sicut argumentum postulabat, videret, accurrisse ferendae opis gratia.

22.1 equorum studio vel praecipue ab ineunte aetate flagravit plurimusque illi sermo, quanquam vetaretur, de circensibus erat; et quondam tractum prasini agitatorem inter condiscipulos querens, obiurgante paedagogo, de Hectore se loqui ementitus est. sed cum inter initia imperii eburneis quadrigis cotidie in abaco luderet, ad omnis etiam minimos circenses e secessu commeabat, primo clam, deinde propalam, ut nemini dubium esset eo die utique affuturum. **22.**2 neque dissimulabat velle se palmarum numerum ampliari; quare spectaculum multiplicatis missibus in serum protrahebatur, ne dominis quidem iam factionum dignantibus nisi ad totius diei cursum greges ducere. mox et ipse aurigare atque etiam spectari saepius voluit positoque in hortis inter servitia et sordidam plebem rudimento universorum se oculis in circo maximo praebuit, aliquo liberto mittente mappam unde magistratus solent. **22.**3 nec contentus harum artium experimenta Romae dedisse, Achaiam, ut diximus, petit hinc maxime motus. instituerant civitates, apud quas musici agones edi solent, omnes citharoedorum coronas ad ipsum mittere. eas adeo grate recipiebat, ut legatos, qui pertulissent, non modo primos admitteret, sed etiam familiaribus epulis interponeret. a quibusdam ex his rogatus ut cantaret super cenam, exceptusque effusius, solos scire audire Graecos solosque se et studiis suis dignos ait. nec profectione dilata, ut primum Cassiopen traiecit, statim ad aram Iovis Cassii cantare auspicatus certamina deinceps obiit omnia.

23.1 nam et quae diversissimorum temporum sunt, cogi in unum annum, quibusdam etiam iteratis, iussit et Olympiae quoque praeter consuetudinem musicum agona commisit. ac ne quid circa haec occupatum avocaret detineretve, cum praesentia eius urbicas res egere a liberto Helio admoneretur, rescripsit his verbis: quamvis nunc tuum consilium sit et votum celeriter reverti me, tamen suadere et optare potius debes, ut Nerone dignus revertar. **23.2** cantante eo ne necessaria quidem causa excedere theatro licitum est. itaque et enixae quaedam in spectaculis dicuntur et multi taedio audiendi laudandique clausis oppidorum portis aut furtim desiluisse de muro aut morte simulata funere elati. quam autem trepide anxieque certaverit, quanta adversariorum aemulatione, quo metu iudicum, vix credi potest. adversarios, quasi plane condicionis eiusdem, observare, captare, infamare secreto, nonnumquam ex occursu maledictis incessere ac, si qui arte praecellerent, conrumpere etiam solebat. **23.3** iudices autem prius quam inciperet reverentissime adloquebatur, omnia se facienda fecisse, sed eventum in manu esse Fortunae; illos ut sapientis et doctos viros fortuita debere excludere; atque, ut auderet hortantibus, aequiore animo recedebat, ac ne sic quidem sine sollicitudine, taciturnitatem pudoremque quorundam pro tristitia et malignitate arguens suspectosque sibi dicens in certando vero ita legi oboediebat,

24.1 ut numquam exscreare ausus sudorem quoque frontis brachio detergeret; atque etiam in tragico quodam actu, cum elapsum baculum cito resumpsisset, pavidus et metuens ne ob delictum certamine summoveretur, non aliter confirmatus est quam adiurante hypocrita non animadversum id inter exsultationes succlamationesque populi. victorem autem se ipse pronuntiabat; qua de causa et praeconio ubique contendit. ac ne cuius alterius hieronicarum memoria aut vestigium exstaret usquam, subverti et unco trahi abicique in latrinas omnium statuas et imagines imperavit. **24.2** aurigavit quoque plurifariam, Olympiis vero etiam decemiugem, quamvis id ipsum in rege Mithradate carmine quodam suo reprehendisset; sed excussus curru ac rursus repositus, cum perdurare non posset, destitit ante decursum; neque eo setius coronatus est. decedens deinde provinciam universam libertate donavit simulque iudices civitate Romana et pecunia grandi. quae beneficia e medio stadio Isthmiorum die sua ipse voce pronuntiavit.

25.1 reversus e Graecia Neapolim, quod in ea primum artem protulerat, albis equis introiit disiecta parte muri, ut mos hieronicarum est; simili modo Antium, inde Albanum, inde Romam; sed et Romam eo curru, quo Augustus olim triumphaverat, et in veste purpurea distinctaque stellis aureis chlamyde coronamque capite gerens Olympiacam, dextra manu Pythiam, praeeunte pompa ceterarum cum titulis, ubi et quos quo cantionum quove fabularum argumento vicisset; sequentibus currum ovantium ritu plausoribus, Augustianos militesque se triumphi eius clamitantibus. **25.2** dehinc diruto circi maximi arcu per Velabrum forumque Palatium et Apollinem petit. incedenti passim victimae caesae sparso per vias identidem croco ingestaeque aves ac lemnisci et bellaria. sacras coronas in cubiculis circum lectos posuit, item statuas suas citharoedico habitu, **25.3** qua nota etiam nummum percussit ac post haec tantum afuit a remittendo laxandoque studio, ut conservandae vocis gratia neque milites umquam, nisi absens aut alio verba pronuntiante, appellaret neque quicquam serio iocove egerit, nisi astante phonasco, qui moneret parceret arteriis ac sudarium ad os applicaret; multisque vel amicitiam suam optulerit vel simultatem indixerit, prout quisque se magis parciusve laudasset.

26.1 petulantiam, libidinem, luxuriam, avaritiam, crudelitatem sensim quidem primo et occulte et velut iuvenili errore exercuit, sed ut tunc quoque dubium nemini foret naturae illa vitia, non aetatis esse. post crepusculum statim adrepto pilleo vel galero popinas inibat circumque vicos vagabatur ludibundus nec sine pernicie tamen, siquidem redeuntis a cena verberare ac repugnantes vulnerare cloacisque demergere assuerat, tabernas etiam effringere et expilare; quintana domi constituta, ubi partae et ad licitationem dividendae praedae pretium absumeretur. **26.2** ac saepe in eius modi rixis oculorum et vitae periculum adiit, a quodam laticlavio, cuius uxorem adtrectaverat, prope ad necem caesus. quare numquam postea publico se illud horae sine tribunis commisit procul et occulte subsequentibus. interdiu quoque clam gestatoria sella delatus in theatrum seditionibus pantomimorum e parte proscaenii superiore signifer simul ac spectator aderat; et cum ad manus ventum esset lapidibusque et subselliorum fragminibus decerneretur, multa et ipse iecit in populum atque etiam praetoris caput consauciavit.

27.1 paulatim vero invalescentibus vitiis iocularia et latebras omisit nullaque dissimulandi cura ad maiora palam erupit. **27.2** epulas a medio die ad mediam noctem protrahebat, refotus saepius calidis piscinis ac tempore aestivo nivatis; cenitabatque nonnumquam et in publico, naumachia praeclusa vel Martio campo vel circo maximo, inter scortorum totius urbis et ambubaiarum ministeria. **27.3** quotiens Ostiam Tiberi deflueret aut Baianum sinum praeternavigaret, dispositae per litora et ripas deversoriae tabernae parabantur insignes ganea et matronarum institorio copas imitantium atque hinc inde hortantium ut appelleret. indicebat et familiaribus cenas, quorum uni mitellita quadragies sestertium constitit, alteri pluris aliquanto rosaria.

28.1 super ingenuorum paedagogia et nuptarum concubinatus Vestali virgini Rubriae vim intulit. Acten libertam paulum afuit quin iusto sibi matrimonio coniungeret, summissis consularibus viris qui regio genere ortam peierarent. puerum Sporum exsectis testibus etiam in muliebrem naturam transfigurare conatus cum dote et flammeo per sollemnia nuptiarum celeberrimo officio deductum ad se pro uxore habuit; exstatque cuiusdam non inscitus iocus bene agi potuisse cum rebus humanis, si Domitius pater talem habuisset uxorem. **28.2** hunc Sporum, Augustarum ornamentis excultum lectica vectum, et circa conventus mercatusque Graeciae ac mox Romae circa Sigillaria comitatus est identidem exosculans. nam matris concubitum appetisse et ab obtrectatoribus eius, ne ferox atque impotens mulier et hoc genere gratiae praevaleret, deterritum nemo dubitavit, utique postquam meretricem, quam fama erat Agrippinae simillimam, inter concubinas recepit. olim etiam quotiens lectica cum matre veheretur, libidinatum inceste ac maculis vestis proditum affirmant.

29.1 suam quidem pudicitiam usque adeo prostituit, ut contaminatis paene omnibus membris novissime quasi genus lusus excogitaret, quo ferae pelle contectus emitteretur e cavea virorumque ac feminarum ad stipitem deligatorum inguina invaderet et, cum affatim desaevisset, conficeretur a Doryphoro liberto; cui etiam, sicut ipsi Sporus, ita ipse denupsit, voces quoque et heiulatus vim patientium virginum imitatus. ex nonnullis comperi persuasissimum habuisse eum neminem hominem pudicum aut ulla corporis parte purum esse, verum plerosque dissimulare vitium et callide optegere; ideoque professis apud se obscaenitatem cetera quoque concessisse delicta.

30.1 divitiarum et pecuniae fructum non alium putabat quam profusionem, sordidos ac deparcos esse quibus impensarum ratio constaret, praelautos vereque magnificos qui abuterentur ac perderent. laudabat mirabaturque avunculum Gaium nullo magis nomine, quam quod ingentis a Tiberio relictas opes in brevi spatio prodegisset. **30.2** quare nec largiendi nec absumendi modum tenuit. in Tiridatem, quod vix credibile videatur, octingena nummum milia diurna erogavit abeuntique super sestertium milies contulit. Menecraten citharoedum et Spiculum murmillonem triumphalium virorum patrimoniis aedibusque donavit. cercopithecum Panerotem faeneratorem et urbanis rusticisque praediis locupletatum prope regio extulit funere. **30.3** nullam vestem bis induit. quadringenis in punctum sestertiis aleam lusit. piscatus est rete aurato et purpura coccoque funibus nexis. numquam minus mille carrucis fecisse iter traditur, soleis mularum argenteis, canusinatis mulionibus, armillata phalerataque Mazacum turba atque cursorum.

31.1 non in alia re tamen damnosior quam in aedificando domum a Palatio Esquilias usque fecit, quam primo transitoriam, mox incendio absumptam restitutamque auream nominavit. de cuius spatio atque cultu suffecerit haec rettulisse. vestibulum eius fuit, in quo colossus CXX pedum staret ipsius effigie; tanta laxitas, ut porticus triplices miliarias haberet; item stagnum maris instar, circumsaeptum aedificiis ad urbium speciem; rura insuper arvis atque vinetis et pascuis silvisque varia, cum multitudine omnis generis pecudum ac ferarum. **31.2** in ceteris partibus cuncta auro lita, distincta gemmis unionumque conchis erant; cenationes laqueatae tabulis eburneis versatilibus, ut flores, fistulatis, ut unguenta desuper spargerentur; praecipua cenationum rotunda, quae perpetuo diebus ac noctibus vice mundi circumageretur; balineae marinis et albulis fluentes aquis. eius modi domum cum absolutam dedicaret, hactenus comprobavit, ut se diceret quasi hominem tandem habitare coepisse. **31.3** praeterea incohabat piscinam a Miseno ad Avernum lacum contectam porticibusque conclusam, quo quidquid totis Baiis calidarum aquarum esset converteretur; fossam ab Averno Ostiam usque, ut navibus nec tamen mari iretur, longitudinis per centum sexaginta milia, latitudinis, qua contrariae quinqueremes commearent. quorum operum perficiendorum gratia quod ubique esset custodiae in Italiam deportari, etiam scelere convictos non nisi ad opus damnari praeceperat. **31.4** ad hunc impendiorum furorem, super fiduciam imperii, etiam spe quadam repentina immensarum et reconditarum opum impulsus est ex indicio equitis R. pro comperto pollicentis thesauros antiquissimae gazae, quos Dido regina fugiens Tyro secum extulisset, esse in Africa vastissimis specubus abditos ac posse erui parvula molientium opera.

32.1 verum ut spes fefellit, destitutus atque ita iam exhaustus et egens ut stipendia quoque militum et commoda veteranorum protrahi ac differri necesse esset, calumniis rapinisque intendit animum. **32.2** ante omnia instituit, ut e libertorum defunctorum bonis pro semisse dextans ei cogeretur, qui sine probabili causa eo nomine essent, quo fuissent ullae familiae quas ipse contingeret; deinde, ut ingratorum in principem testamenta ad fiscum pertinerent, ac ne impune esset studiosis iuris, qui scripsissent vel dictassent ea; tunc ut lege maiestatis facta dictaque omnia, quibus modo delator non deesset, tenerentur. **32.3** revocavit et praemia coronarum, quae umquam sibi civitates in certaminibus detulissent. et cum interdixisset usum amethystini ac Tyrii coloris summisissetque qui nundinarum die pauculas uncias venderet, praeclusit cunctos negotiatores. quin etiam inter canendum animadversam matronam in spectaculis vetita purpura cultam demonstrasse procuratoribus suis dicitur detractamque ilico non veste modo sed et bonis exuit. **32.4** nulli delegavit officium ut non adiceret: scis quid mihi opus sit, et: hoc agamus, ne quis quicquam habeat. ultimo templis compluribus dona detraxit simulacraque ex auro vel argento fabricata conflavit, in iis Penatium deorum, quae mox Galba restituit.

33.1 parricidia et caedes a Claudio exorsus est; cuius necis etsi non auctor, at conscius fuit, neque dissimulanter, ut qui boletos, in quo cibi genere venenum is acceperat, quasi deorum cibum posthac proverbio Graeco conlaudare sit solitus. certe omnibus rerum verborumque contumeliis mortuum insectatus est, modo stultitiae modo saevitiae arguens; nam et morari eum desisse inter homines producta prima syllaba iocabatur multaque decreta et constituta, ut insipientis atque deliri, pro irritis habuit; denique bustum eius consaepiri nisi humili levique maceria neglexit. **33.2** Britannicum non minus aemulatione vocis, quae illi iucundior suppetebat, quam metu ne quandoque apud hominum gratiam paterna memoria praevaleret, veneno adgressus est. quod acceptum a quadam Lucusta, venenariorum indice, cum opinione tardius cederet ventre modo Britannici moto, accersitam mulierem sua manu verberavit arguens pro veneno remedium dedisse; excusantique minus datum ad occultandam facinoris invidiam: sane, inquit, legem Iuliam timeo, coegitque se coram in cubiculo quam posset velocissimum ac praesentaneum coquere. **33.3** deinde in haedo expertus, postquam is quinque horas protraxit, iterum ac saepius recoctum porcello obiecit; quo statim exanimato inferri in triclinium darique cenanti secum Britannico imperavit. et cum ille ad primum gustum concidisset, comitiali morbo ex consuetudine correptum apud convivas ementitus postero die raptim inter maximos imbres tralaticio extulit funere. Lucustae pro navata opera impunitatem praediaque ampla, sed et discipulos dedit.

34.1 matrem facta dictaque sua exquirentem acerbius et corrigentem hactenus primo gravabatur, ut invidia identidem oneraret quasi cessurus imperio Rhodumque abiturus, mox et honore omni et potestate privavit abductaque militum et Germanorum statione contubernio quoque ac Palatio expulit; neque in divexanda quicquam pensi habuit, summissis qui et Romae morantem litibus et in secessu quiescentem per convicia et iocos terra marique praetervehentes inquietarent. **34.2** verum minis eius ac violentia territus perdere statuit; et cum ter veneno temptasset sentiretque antidotis praemunitam, lacunaria, quae noctu super dormientem laxata machina deciderent, paravit. hoc consilio per conscios parum celato solutilem navem, cuius vel naufragio vel camarae ruina periret, commentus est atque ita reconciliatione simulata iucundissimis litteris Baias evocavit ad sollemnia Quinquatruum simul celebranda; datoque negotio trierarchis, qui liburnicam qua advecta erat velut fortuito concursu confringerent, protraxit convivium repetentique Baulos in locum corrupti navigii machinosum illud optulit, hilare prosecutus atque in digressu papillas quoque exosculatus. **34.3** reliquum temporis cum magna trepidatione vigilavit opperiens coeptorum exitum. sed ut diversa omnia nandoque evasisse eam comperit, inops consilii L. Agerinum libertum eius salvam et incolumem cum gaudio nuntiantem, abiecto clam iuxta pugione ut percussorem sibi subornatum arripi constringique iussit, matrem occidi, quasi deprehensum crimen voluntaria morte vitasset. **34.4** adduntur his atrociora nec incertis auctoribus: ad visendum interfectae cadaver accurrisse, contrectasse membra, alia vituperasse, alia laudasse, sitique interim oborta bibisse. neque tamen conscientiam sceleris, quanquam et militum et senatus populique gratulationibus confirmaretur, aut statim aut umquam postea ferre potuit, saepe confessus exagitari se materna specie verberibusque Furiarum ac taedis ardentibus. quin et facto per Magos sacro evocare Manes exorare temptavit.

peregrinatione quidem Graeciae et Eleusinis sacris, quorum initiatione impii et scelerati voce praeconis summoventur, interesse non ausus est. **34.5** iunxit parricidio matris amitae necem. quam cum ex duritie alvi cubantem visitaret, et illa tractans lanuginem eius, ut assolet, iam grandis natu per blanditias forte dixisset: simul hanc excepero, mori volo, conversus ad proximos confestim se positurum velut irridens ait, praecepitque medicis ut largius purgarent aegram; necdum defunctae bona invasit suppresso testamento, ne quid abscederet.

35.1 uxores praeter Octaviam duas postea duxit, Poppaeam Sabinam quaestorio patre natam et equiti R. antea nuptam, deinde Statiliam Messalinam Tauri bis consulis ac triumphalis abneptem. qua ut poteretur, virum eius Atticum Vestinum consulem in honore ipso trucidavit. Octaviae consuetudinem cito aspernatus, corripientibus amicis sufficere illi debere respondit uxoria ornamenta. **35.2** eandem mox saepe frustra strangulare meditatus dimisit ut sterilem, sed improbante divortium populo nec parcente conviciis, etiam relegavit, denique occidit sub crimine adulteriorum adeo inpudenti falsoque, ut in quaestione pernegantibus cunctis Anicetum paedagogum suum indicem subiecerit, qui dolo stupratam a se fateretur. **35.3** Poppaeam duodecimo die post divortium Octaviae in matrimonium acceptam dilexit unice; et tamen ipsam quoque ictu calcis occidit, quod se ex aurigatione sero reversum gravida et aegra conviciis incesserat. ex hac filiam tulit Claudiam Augustam amisitque admodum infantem. **35.4** nullum adeo necessitudinis genus est, quod non scelere perculerit. Antoniam Claudi filiam, recusantem post Poppaeae mortem nuptias suas, quasi molitricem novarum rerum interemit; similiter inter ceteros aut affinitate aliqua sibi aut propinquitate coniunctos; in quibus Aulum Plautium iuvenem, quem cum ante mortem per vim conspurcasset: eat nunc, inquit, mater mea et successorem meum osculetur, iactans dilectum ab ea et ad spem imperii impulsum. **35.5** privignum Rufrium Crispinum Poppaea natum, impuberem adhuc, quia ferebatur ducatus et imperia ludere, mergendum mari, dum piscaretur, servis ipsius demandavit. Tuscum nutricis filium relegavit, quod in procuratione Aegypti balineis in adventum suum exstructis lavisset. Senecam praeceptorem ad necem compulit, quamvis saepe commeatum petenti bonisque cedenti persancte iurasset suspectum se frustra periturumque potius quam nociturum ei. Burro praefecto remedium ad fauces pollicitus toxicum misit. libertos divites et senes, olim adoptionis mox dominationis suae fautores atque rectores, veneno partim cibis partim potionibus indito intercepit.

36.1 nec minore saevitia foris et in exteros grassatus est. stella crinita, quae summis potestatibus exitium portendere vulgo putatur, per continuas noctes oriri coeperat. anxius ea re, ut ex Balbillo astrologo didicit, solere reges talia ostenta caede aliqua illustri expiare atque a semet in capita procerum depellere, nobilissimo cuique exitium destinavit; enimvero multo magis et quasi per iustam causam duabus coniurationibus provulgatis, quarum prior maiorque Pisoniana Romae, posterior Viniciana Beneventi conflata atque detecta est. **36.2** coniurati e vinculis triplicium catenarum dixere causam, cum quidam ultro crimen faterentur, nonnulli etiam imputarent, tamquam aliter illi non possent nisi morte succurrere dedecorato flagitiis omnibus. damnatorum liberi urbe pulsi enectique veneno aut fame; constat quosdam cum paedagogis et capsariis uno prandio pariter necatos, alios diurnum victum prohibitos quaerere.

37.1 nullus posthac adhibitus dilectus aut modus interimendi quoscumque libuisset quacumque de causa. sed ne de pluribus referam, Salvidieno Orfito obiectum est quod tabernas tres de domo sua circa forum civitatibus ad stationem locasset, Cassio Longino iuris consulto ac luminibus orbato, quod in vetere gentili stemmate C. Cassi percussoris Caesaris imagines retinuisset, Paeto Thraseae tristior et paedagogi vultus. **37.2** mori iussis non amplius quam horarum spatium dabat; ac ne quid morae interveniret, medicos admovebat qui cunctantes continuo curarent: ita enim vocabatur venas mortis gratia incidere. creditur etiam polyphago cuidam Aegypti generis crudam carnem et quidquid daretur mandere assueto, concupisse vivos homines laniandos absumendosque obicere. **37.3** elatus inflatusque tantis velut successibus negavit quemquam principum scisse quid sibi liceret, multasque nec dubias significationes saepe iecit, ne reliquis quidem se parsurum senatoribus, eumque ordinem sublaturum quandoque e re p. ac provincias et exercitus equiti R. ac libertis permissurum. certe neque adveniens neque proficiscens quemquam osculo impertiit ac ne resalutatione quidem; et in auspicando opere Isthmi magna frequentia clare ut sibi ac populo R. bene res verteret optavit dissimulata senatus mentione.

38.1 sed nec populo aut moenibus patriae pepercit. dicente quodam in sermone communi

ἐμοῦ θανόντος γαῖα μειχθήτω πυρί,

immo, inquit, ἐμοῦ ζῶντος, planeque ita fecit. nam quasi offensus deformitate veterum aedificiorum et angustiis flexurisque vicorum, incendit urbem tam palam, ut plerique consulares cubicularios eius cum stuppa taedaque in praediis suis deprehensos non attigerint, et quaedam horrea circa domum Auream, quorum spatium maxime desiderabat, ut bellicis machinis labefacta atque inflammata sint, quod saxeo muro constructa erant. **38.2** per sex dies septemque noctes ea clade saevitum est ad monumentorum bustorumque deversoria plebe compulsa. tunc praeter immensum numerum insularum domus priscorum ducum arserunt hostilibus adhuc spoliis adornatae deorumque aedes ab regibus ac deinde Punicis et Gallicis bellis votae dedicataeque, et quidquid visendum atque memorabile ex antiquitate duraverat. hoc incendium e turre Maecenatiana prospectans laetusque flammae, ut aiebat, pulchritudine Halosin Ilii in illo suo scaenico habitu decantavit. **38.**3 ac ne non hinc quoque quantum posset praedae et manubiarum invaderet, pollicitus cadaverum et ruderum gratuitam egestionem nemini ad reliquias rerum suarum adire permisit; conlationibusque non receptis modo verum et efflagitatis provincias privatorumque census prope exhausit.

39.1 accesserunt tantis ex principe malis probrisque quaedam et fortuita: pestilentia unius autumni, quo triginta funerum milia in rationem Libitinae venerunt; clades Britannica, qua duo praecipua oppida magna civium sociorumque caede direpta sunt; ignominia ad Orientem legionibus in Armenia sub iugum missis aegreque Syria retenta. mirum et vel praecipue notabile inter haec fuerit nihil eum patientius quam maledicta et convicia hominum tulisse, neque in ullos leniorem quam qui se dictis aut carminibus lacessissent exstitisse. **39.**2 multa Graece Latineque proscripta aut vulgata sunt, sicut illa:

Νέρων Ὀρέστης Ἀλκμέων μητροκτόνος.

νεόψηφον· Νέρων ἰδίαν μητέρα ἀπέκτεινε.

quis negat Aeneae magna de stirpe Neronem?
  sustulit hic matrem, sustulit ille patrem.

dum tendit citharam noster, dum cornua Parthus,
  noster erit Paean, ille Hecatebeletes.

Roma domus fiet: Veios migrate, Quirites,
  si non et Veios occupat ista domus.

sed neque auctores requisiit et quosdam per indicem delatos ad senatum adfici graviore poena prohibuit. **39.**3 transeuntem eum Isidorus Cynicus in publico clara voce corripuerat, quod Naupli mala bene cantitaret, sua bona male disponeret; et Datus Atellanarum histrio in cantico quodam

ὑγίαινε πάτερ, ὑγίαινε μῆτερ

ita demonstraverat, ut bibentem natantemque faceret, exitum scilicet Claudi Agrippinaeque significans, et in novissima clausula

Orcus vobis ducit pedes

senatum gestu notaret. histrionem et philosophum Nero nihil amplius quam urbe Italiaque summovit, vel contemptu omnis infamiae vel ne fatendo dolorem irritaret ingenia.

40.1 talem principem paulo minus quattuordecim annos perpessus terrarum orbis tandem destituit, initium facientibus Gallis duce Iulio Vindice, qui tum eam provinciam pro praetore optinebat. **40.**2 praedictum a mathematicis Neroni olim erat fore ut quandoque destitueretur; unde illa vox eius celeberrima: τὸ τέχνον ἡμᾶς διατρέφει, quo maiore scilicet venia meditaretur citharoedicam artem, principi sibi gratam, privato necessariam. spoponderant tamen quidam destituto Orientis dominationem, nonnulli nominatim regnum Hierosolymorum, plures omnis pristinae fortunae restitutionem. cui spei pronior, Britannia Armeniaque amissa ac rursus utraque recepta, defunctum se fatalibus malis existimabat. **40.3** ut vero consulto Delphis Apolline septuagensimum ac tertium annum cavendum sibi audivit, quasi eo demum obiturus, ac nihil coniectans de aetate Galbae, tanta fiducia non modo senectam sed etiam perpetuam singularemque concepit felicitatem, ut amissis naufragio pretiosissimis rebus non dubitaverit inter suos dicere pisces eas sibi relaturos. **40.4** Neapoli de motu Galliarum cognovit die ipso quo matrem occiderat, adeoque lente ac secure tulit ut gaudentis etiam suspicionem praeberet tamquam occasione nata spoliandarum iure belli opulentissimarum provinciarum; statimque in gymnasium progressus certantis athletas effusissimo studio spectavit. cenae quoque tempore interpellatus tumultuosioribus litteris hactenus excanduit, ut malum iis qui descissent minaretur. denique per octo continuos dies non rescribere cuiquam, non mandare quid aut praecipere conatus rem silentio obliteravit.

41.1 edictis tandem Vindicis contumeliosis et frequentibus permotus senatum epistula in ultionem sui reique publicae adhortatus est, excusato languore faucium, propter quem non adesset. nihil autem aeque doluit, quam ut malum se citharoedum increpitum ac pro Nerone Ahenobarbum appellatum; et nomen quidem gentile, quod sibi per contumeliam exprobraretur, resumpturum se professus est deposito adoptivo, cetera convicia, ut falsa, non alio argumento refellebat, quam quod etiam inscitia sibi tanto opere elaboratae perfectaeque a se artis obiceretur, singulos subinde rogitans, nossentne quemquam praestantiorem. **41.2** sed urgentibus aliis super alios nuntiis Romam praetrepidus rediit: leviterque modo in itinere frivolo auspicio mente recreata, cum adnotasset insculptum monumento militem Gallum ab equite R. oppressum trahi crinibus, ad eam speciem exsiluit gaudio caelumque adoravit. ac ne tunc quidem aut senatu aut populo coram appellato quosdam e primoribus viris domum evocavit transactaque raptim consultatione reliquam diei partem per organa hydraulica novi et ignoti generis circumduxit, ostendensque singula, de ratione ac difficultate cuiusque disserens, iam se etiam prolaturum omnia in theatrum affirmavit, si per Vindicem liceat.

42.1 postquam deinde etiam Galbam et Hispanias descivisse cognovit, conlapsus animoque male facto diu sine voce et prope intermortuus iacuit, utque resipiit, veste discissa, capite converberato, actum de se pronuntiavit consolantique nutriculae et aliis quoque iam principibus similia accidisse memoranti, se vero praeter ceteros inaudita et incognita pati respondit, qui summum imperium vivus amitteret. **42.2** nec eo setius quicquam ex consuetudine luxus atque desidiae omisit vel inminuit; quin immo, cum prosperi quiddam ex provinciis nuntiatum esset, super abundantissimam cenam iocularia in defectionis duces carmina lasciveque modulata, quae vulgo notuerunt, etiam gesticulatus est; ac spectaculis theatri clam inlatus cuidam scaenico placenti nuntium misit abuti eum occupationibus suis.

43.1 initio statim tumultus multa et inmania, verum non abhorrentia a natura sua creditur destinasse: successores percussoresque summittere exercitus et provincias regentibus, quasi conspiratis idemque et unum sentientibus; quidquid ubique exsulum, quidquid in urbe hominum Gallicanorum esset contrucidare, illos ne desciscentibus adgregarentur, hos ut conscios popularium suorum atque fautores; Gallias exercitibus diripiendas permittere; senatum universum veneno per convivia necare; urbem incendere feris in populum immissis, quo difficilius defenderentur. **43.**2 sed absterritus non tam paenitentia quam perficiendi desperatione credensque expeditionem necessariam, consules ante tempus privavit honore atque in utriusque locum solus iniit consulatum, quasi fatale esset non posse Gallias debellari nisi a consule. ac susceptis fascibus cum post epulas triclinio digrederetur, innixus umeris familiarium affirmavit, simul ac primum provinciam attigisset, inermem se in conspectum exercituum proditurum nec quicquam aliud quam fleturum, revocatisque ad paenitentiam defectoribus insequenti die laetum inter laetos cantaturum epinicia, quae iam nunc sibi componi oporteret.

44.1 in praeparanda expeditione primam curam habuit deligendi vehicula portandis scaenicis organis concubinasque, quas secum educeret, tondendi ad virilem modum et securibus peltisque Amazonicis instruendi. mox tribus urbanas ad sacramentum citavit ac nullo idoneo respondente certum dominis servorum numerum indixit; nec nisi ex tota cuiusque familia probatissimos, ne dispensatoribus quidem aut amanuensibus exceptis, recepit. **44.**2 partem etiam census omnes ordines conferre iussit et insuper inquilinos privatarum aedium atque insularum pensionem annuam repraesentare fisco; exegitque ingenti fastidio et acerbitate nummum asperum, argentum pustulatum, aurum ad obrussam, ut plerique omnem collationem palam recusarent, consensu flagitantes a delatoribus potius revocanda praemia quaecumque cepissent.

45.1 ex annonae quoque caritate lucranti adcrevit invidia; nam et forte accidit, ut in publica fame Alexandrina navis nuntiaretur pulverem luctatoribus aulicis advexisse. **45.**2 quare omnium in se odio incitato nihil contumeliarum defuit quin subiret. statuae eius a vertice cirrus appositus est cum inscriptione Graeca: nunc demum agona esse, et traderet tandem. alterius collo ascopera deligata simulque titulus: ego quid potui? sed tu culleum meruisti. ascriptum et columnis, etiam Gallos eum cantando excitasse. iam noctibus iurgia cum servis plerique simulantes crebro Vindicem poscebant.

46.1 terrebatur ad hoc evidentibus portentis somniorum et auspiciorum et

Suetonius: Nero

ominum, cum veteribus tum novis. numquam antea somniare solitus occisa demum matre vidit per quietem navem sibi regenti extortum gubernaculum trahique se ab Octavia uxore in artissimas tenebras et modo pinnatarum formicarum multitudine oppleri, modo a simulacris gentium ad Pompei theatrum dedicatarum circumiri arcerique progressu; asturconem, quo maxime laetabatur, posteriore corporis parte in simiae speciem transfiguratum ac tantum capite integro hinnitus edere canoros. **46.2** de Mausoleo, sponte foribus patefactis, exaudita vox est nomine eum cientis. Kal. Ian. exornati Lares in ipso sacrificii apparatu conciderunt; auspicanti Sporus anulum muneri optulit, cuius gemmae scalptura erat Proserpinae raptus; votorum nuncupatione, magna iam ordinum frequentia, vix repertae Capitolii claves. **46.3** cum ex oratione eius, qua in Vindicem perorabat, recitaretur in senatu daturos poenas sceleratos ac brevi dignum exitum facturos, conclamatum est ab universis: tu facies, Auguste. observatum etiam fuerat novissimam fabulam cantasse eum publice Oedipodem exsulem atque in hoc desisse versu:

θανεῖν μ᾽ ἄνωγε σύγγαμος, μήτηρ, πάτηρ.

47.1 nuntiata interim etiam ceterorum exercituum defectione litteras prandenti sibi redditas concerpsit, mensam subvertit, duos scyphos gratissimi usus, quos Homerios a caelatura carminum Homeri vocabat, solo inlisit ac sumpto a Lucusta veneno et in auream pyxidem condito transiit in hortos Servilianos, ubi praemissis libertorum fidissimis Ostiam ad classem praeparandam tribunos centurionesque praetorii de fugae societate temptavit. **47.2** sed partim tergiversantibus, partim aperte detrectantibus, uno vero etiam proclamante:

usque adeone mori miserum est?

varie agitavit, Parthosne an Galbam supplex peteret, an atratus prodiret in publicum proque rostris quanta maxima posset miseratione veniam praeteritorum precaretur, ac ni flexisset animos, vel Aegypti praefecturam concedi sibi oraret. inventus est postea in scrinio eius hac de re sermo formatus; sed deterritum putant, ne prius quam in forum perveniret discerperetur. **47.3** sic cogitatione in posterum diem dilata ad mediam fere noctem excitatus, ut comperit stationem militum recessisse, prosiluit e lecto misitque circum amicos, et quia nihil a quoquam renuntiabatur, ipse cum paucis hospitia singulorum adiit. verum clausis omnium foribus, respondente nullo, in cubiculum rediit, unde iam et custodes diffugerant, direptis etiam stragulis, amota et pyxide veneni; ac statim Spiculum murmillonem vel quemlibet alium percussorem, cuius manu periret, requisiit et nemine reperto: ergo ego, inquit, nec amicum habeo nec inimicum? procurritque, quasi praecipitaturus se in Tiberim.

48.1 sed revocato rursus impetu aliquid secretioris latebrae ad colligendum

18

animum desideravit, et offerente Phaonte liberto suburbanum suum inter
Salariam et Nomentanam viam circa quartum miliarium, ut erat nudo pede atque
tunicatus, paenulam obsoleti coloris superinduit adopertoque capite et ante
faciem optento sudario equum inscendit, quattuor solis comitantibus, inter quos
et Sporus erat. **48.**2 statimque tremore terrae et fulgure adverso pavefactus audiit
e proximis castris clamorem militum et sibi adversa et Galbae prospera ominantium,
etiam ex obviis viatoribus quendam dicentem: hi Neronem persequuntur, alium
sciscitantem: ecquid in urbe novi de Nerone? equo autem ex odore abiecti in via
cadaveris consternato, detecta facie agnitus est a quodam missicio praetoriano et
salutatus. **48.3** ut ad deverticulum ventum est, dimissis equis inter fruticeta ac
vepres per harundineti semitam aegre nec nisi strata sub pedibus veste ad aversum
villae parietem evasit. ibi hortante eodem Phaonte, ut interim in specum egestae
harenae concederet, negavit se vivum sub terram iturum, ac parumper commoratus,
dum clandestinus ad villam introitus pararetur, aquam ex subiecta lacuna poturus
manu hausit et: haec est, inquit, Neronis decocta. **48.4** dein divolsa sentibus
paenula traiectos surculos rasit, atque ita quadripes per angustias effossae cavernae
receptus in proximam cellam decubuit super lectum modica culcita, vetere pallio
strato, instructum; fameque et iterum siti interpellante panem quidem sordidum
oblatum aspernatus est, aquae autem tepidae aliquantum bibit.

    49.1 tunc uno quoque hinc inde instante ut quam primum se impendentibus
contumeliis eriperet, scrobem coram fieri imperavit dimensus ad corporis sui
modulum, componique simul, si qua invenirentur, frustra marmoris et aquam
simul ac ligna conferri curando mox cadaveri, flens ad singula atque identidem
dictitans: qualis artifex pereo! **49.2** inter moras perlatos a cursore Phaonti
codicillos praeripuit legitque se hostem a senatu iudicatum et quaeri, ut puniatur
more maiorum, interrogavitque quale id genus esset poenae; et cum comperisset
nudi hominis cervicem inseri furcae, corpus virgis ad necem caedi, conterritus
duos pugiones, quos secum extulerat, arripuit temptataque utriusque acie rursus
condidit, causatus nondum adesse fatalem horam. **49.3** ac modo Sporum hort-
abatur ut lamentari ac plangere inciperet, modo orabat ut se aliquis ad mortem
capessendam exemplo iuvaret; interdum segnitiem suam his verbis increpabat:
vivo deformiter, turpiter – οὐ πρέπει Νέρωνι, οὐ πρέπει – νήφειν δεῖ ἐν τοῖς
τοιούτοις – ἄγε ἔγειρε σεαυτόν. iamque equites appropinquabant, quibus
praeceptum erat ut vivum eum adtraherent. quod ut sensit, trepidanter effatus:

ἵππων μ᾽ ὠκυπόδων ἀμφὶ κτύπος οὔατα βάλλει

ferrum iugulo adegit iuvante Epaphrodito a libellis. **49:4** semianimisque adhuc
irrumpenti centurioni et paenula ad vulnus adposita in auxilium se venisse simulanti
non aliud respondit quam: sero; et: haec est fides. atque in ea voce defecit,
exstantibus rigentibusque oculis usque ad horrorem formidinemque visentium. nihil

19

prius aut magis a comitibus exegerat quam ne potestas cuiquam capitis sui fieret, sed ut quoquo modo totus cremaretur. permisit hoc Icelus, Galbae libertus, non multo ante vinculis exsolutus, in quae primo tumultu coniectus fuerat.

50.1 funeratus est impensa ducentorum milium, stragulis albis auro intextis, quibus usus Kal. Ian. fuerat. reliquias Ecloge et Alexandria nutrices cum Acte concubina gentili Domitiorum monimento condiderunt, quod prospicitur e campo Martio impositum colli Hortulorum. in eo monimento solium porphyretici marmoris, superstante Lunensi ara, circumsaeptum est lapide Thasio.

51.1 statura fuit prope iusta, corpore maculoso et fetido, subflavo capillo, vultu pulchro magis quam venusto, oculis caesis et hebetioribus, cervice obesa, ventre proiecto, gracillimis cruribus, valitudine prospera: nam qui luxuriae immoderatissimae esset, ter omnino per quattuordecim annos languit, atque ita ut neque vino neque consuetudine reliqua abstineret; circa cultum habitumque adeo pudendus, ut comam semper in gradus formatam peregrinatione Achaica etiam pone verticem summiserit ac plerumque synthesinam indutus ligato circum collum sudario prodierit in publicum sine cinctu et discalciatus.

52.1 liberalis disciplinas omnis fere puer attigit. sed a philosophia eum mater avertit monens imperaturo contrariam esse; a cognitione veterum oratorum Seneca praeceptor, quo diutius in admiratione sui detineret. itaque ad poeticam pronus carmina libenter ac sine labore composuit nec, ut quidam putant, aliena pro suis edidit. venere in manus meas pugillares libellique cum quibusdam notissimis versibus ipsius chirographo scriptis, ut facile appareret non tralatos aut dictante aliquo exceptos, sed plane quasi a cogitante atque generante exaratos; ita multa et deleta et inducta et superscripta inerant. habuit et pingendi fingendique non mediocre studium.

53.1 maxime autem popularitate efferebatur, omnium aemulus, qui quoquo modo animum vulgi moverent. exiit opinio post scaenicas coronas proximo lustro descensurum eum ad Olympia inter athletas; nam et luctabatur assidue nec aliter certamina gymnica tota Graecia spectaverat quam brabeutarum more in stadio humi assidens ac, si qua paria longius recessissent, in medium manibus suis protrahens. destinaverat etiam, quia Apollinem cantu, Solem aurigando aequiperare existimaretur, imitari et Herculis facta; praeparatumque leonem aiunt, quem vel clava vel brachiorum nexibus in amphitheatri harena spectante populo nudus elideret.

54.1 sub exitu quidem vitae palam voverat, si sibi incolumis status permansisset, proditurum se partae victoriae ludis etiam hydraulam et choraulam et utricularium ac novissimo die histrionem saltaturumque Vergili Turnum. et sunt qui tradant Paridem histrionem occisum ab eo quasi gravem adversarium.

55.1 erat illi aeternitatis perpetuaeque famae cupido, sed inconsulta. ideoque multis rebus ac locis vetere appellatione detracta novam indixit ex suo nomine, mensem quoque Aprilem Neroneum appellavit; destinaverat et Romam Neropolim nuncupare.

56.1 religionum usque quaque contemptor, praeter unius Deae Syriae, hanc mox ita sprevit ut urina contaminaret, alia superstitione captus, in qua sola pertinacissime haesit, siquidem imagunculam puellarem, cum quasi remedium insidiarum a plebeio quodam et ignoto muneri accepisset, detecta confestim coniuratione pro summo numine trinisque in die sacrificiis colere perseveravit volebatque credi monitione eius futura praenoscere. ante paucos quam periret menses attendit et extispicio nec umquam litavit.

57.1 obiit tricensimo et secundo aetatis anno, die quo quondam Octaviam interemerat, tantumque gaudium publice praebuit, ut plebs pilleata tota urbe discurreret. et tamen non defuerunt qui per longum tempus vernis aestivisque floribus tumulum eius ornarent ac modo imagines praetextatas in rostris proferrent, modo edicta quasi viventis et brevi magno inimicorum malo reversuri. **57.**2 quin etiam Vologaesus Parthorum rex missis ad senatum legatis de instauranda societate hoc etiam magno opere oravit, ut Neronis memoria coleretur. denique cum post viginti annos adulescente me exstitisset condicionis incertae qui se Neronem esse iactaret, tam favorabile nomen eius apud Parthos fuit, ut vehementer adiutus et vix redditus sit.

Commentary

1.1

Ex gente Domitia...Calvinorum: the *gens Domitia* was plebeian until it was raised to patrician rank by Augustus (1.2 below). The Domitii Calvini first provided a consul in 332 BC and another in 304 BC; thereafter they remained in obscurity until the praetor M. Domitius Calvinus in 74 BC and his son Cn. Domitius Calvinus, consul for the second time in 40 BC. The family then disappeared from history.

Ahenobarbi auctorem...rutila barba: the father and the grandfather of the consul of 191 BC (1.2 below) were both called Lucius, and if Suetonius is correct about the succession of *praenomina* in the family, it emerged later than the Domitii Calvini and lacked their early distinction, since it must have been the great-grandfather of the first consul who was the *auctor cognominis*. The apparition of the godlike twins (Castor and Pollux) to a Lucius Domitius is a reference to the battle of Lake Regillus between Rome and the Latins, traditionally in 496 BC (see Livy, 2.19-20), and so well known that Suetonius can be oblique. The association of a Domitius with it was doubtless an invention of the late republican era when legendary origins became a fashion among the nobility.

1.2

functi autem...patricios adlecti: Suetonius only counts the consulships held before the battle of Actium (31 BC). They occurred in 191, 162, 122, 96, 94, 54 and 32 BC. Subsequently Nero's grandfather was consul in 16 BC and his father in AD 32. The triumph was that of Cn. Domitius for the victory over the Arverni, Saluvii and Allobroges, and took place probably in 118 BC following his proconsulship; he went on to hold the censorship in 115 BC, as did his son in 92 BC. The family was raised to patrician rank by Augustus, probably in 29 BC. The record of the Domitii was in one respect even more remarkable than Suetonius indicates, since successive consulships down to Nero were held in direct line from father to son (the consul of 94 BC being the brother of the consul of 96 BC). The physical characteristic which gave the family its name is attested for Nero (51 below). Suetonius gives a similar list of honours and victories achieved by the Claudian ancestors of Tiberius in his life of that emperor.

2.1

atavus eius...ad populum transtulit: *atavus*, here correctly the father of a great-great grandfather. Cn. Domitius Ahenobarbus, the consul of 96 and censor of 92 BC was tribune of the plebs in 104 BC. It had been general practice, though not obligatory, for the priestly colleges to co-opt new members from the family of a deceased *pontifex*. The *lex Domitia de sacerdotiis* laid down that replacements in the pontifical colleges should be nominated by the colleges but elected by 17 of the 35 tribes chosen by lot. He was himself elected *pontifex maximus* the year following the passing of his law. In spite of the superficially popular character of the law, he was in general a solid supporter of the *optimates*.

at in consulatu...triumphi prosequente: Suetonius has confused the victor over the tribes of Gallia Narbonensis with his son whom he has just mentioned (and was not the only ancient author to do so, no doubt because they both had the *praenomen* Gnaeus). Another mistake is that the victory over the Allobroges and Arverni in 121 BC occurred in his proconsulship, not consulship.

2.2

in hunc...plumbeum esse: Suetonius here returns to Nero's *atavus*. L. Licinius Crassus was the famous orator much admired by Cicero, and colleague of Cn. Domitius in the censorship of 92 BC. Their quarrel was a bitter one, though probably based on no more than difference of personality. Pliny the Elder (*N.H.* 27.2-4) has a story of Domitius' criticism of Crassus' wealth and luxurious way of life.

huius filius...numero habendos (3): L. Domitius Ahenobarbus held the praetorship in 58 BC. His hostility to Caesar was pronounced and may have been partly due to Caesar's growing popularity with the city population among whom the Domitii had their own influential position and partly to resentment at Caesar's activity in Gaul, where the Domitii had claimed patronage and influence since 121 BC. In addition, he married Cato's sister. The proposal that Caesar should be removed from his command in Gaul was in fact part of Domitius' election programme of 56 BC in the consular elections for 55 BC. However, at the conference at Luca, Caesar, Pompey and Crassus renewed their compact and prevented the threat from materialising. Domitius had to wait another year for his consulship (54 BC) and made no move against Caesar during it. He remained one of the most ruthless opponents of Caesar but his arrogance made him almost as much disliked by followers of Pompey in the civil war. His attitude towards the 'neutrals' is also mentioned in Caesar, *B.C.* 3.83. Domitius was pursued and killed by Caesar's cavalry when in flight from the battle of Pharsalus. However, Lucan (2.478 ff.) treats his defeat at Corfinium sympathetically.

3.1

Reliquit filium...transfugisse iactavit: Cn. Domitius Ahenobarbus, consul in 32 BC. He fought on the Republican side against Caesar with whom he never formally made peace. He was certainly condemned as a participant in Caesar's murder by the *Lex Pedia* (Appian, *B.C.* 5.55) but, in spite of Cicero's assertion (*Phil.* 2.27.30), Suetonius may be correct in declaring his innocence (Appian *B.C.* 5.61.62). The *Lex Pedia* was passed in 43 BC in the consulship of Caesar's nephews, Q. Pedius and Octavian, created consuls to replace Hirtius and Pansa, killed at Mutina. As the nephew of Cato he was related to Brutus through Brutus' marriage to Cato's daughter in 45 BC; Cassius was married to Brutus' half-sister. He commanded the Republican fleet in the eastern Mediterranean, raising it at one time to over 200 ships, and he continued even after the deaths of Brutus and Cassius. In 40 BC he surrendered to Antony and was pardoned by Octavian in 39 BC in the negotiations between Antony, Octavian and Sextus Pompeius at Misenum. However, he remained with Antony in the east, governing Bithynia (and taking part in Antony's Parthian war in 36 BC), until his consulship in 32 BC. This occurred when relations between Antony and Octavian were at breaking point and Domitius returned at once to the east. His hostility to Cleopatra is confirmed by Plutarch (*Antony* 56) but only Suetonius has the suggestion that some wanted to make him leader of the anti-Octavian cause. His death soon after his flight seems to confirm the story of his illness.

4.1

ex hoc Domitius...edicto coercere: in spite of the active leadership in the Republican cause of both his father and his grandfather, L. Domitius Ahenobarbus was more honoured and successful under Augustus than any other member of those noble families which survived the civil wars. His closeness to the imperial house was marked by his marriage to the elder Antonia, elder daughter of Antony and Octavia, Augustus' sister. The betrothal dated to 37 BC in Antonia's infancy, when Antony and Octavian were at peace, but the arrangement was maintained after Actium and the marriage took place during the 20s BC, perhaps not long after Domitius and his *gens* were given patrician rank. His aedileship was in 22 BC, praetorship before 18 BC, and consulship in 16 BC. He was proconsul of Africa in 12 BC and then played a prominent part in Augustus' German wars. He commanded the army in Illyricum from c. 6-1 BC taking Roman arms beyond the Elbe for the first time, for which he was awarded the *ornamenta triumphalia*. He then commanded the army on the Rhine for some two years.

For the fictitious sale to the *familiae emptor* under the testamentary procedure *per aes et libram*, see *PW* V (A) 1. 987; Augustus wrote his will the year before his death in 14, and Domitius as *familiae emptor* had a position analogous to an executor. *Familia*, here 'estate' in the legal sense.

Suetonius is the only source for the stories of his expertise at chariot racing, his introduction of *equites* and women on the stage, and his *saevitia*, all of which rather obviously foreshadow actions or personality traits of Nero, and illustrate what Suetonius has said (1.2 above), *ut tamen vitia cuiusque quasi tradita et ingenita rettulerit.* Plancus, consul in 42 BC, was not censor until 20 BC, after the aedileship of Domitius, but for an aedile to insult an ex-consul was just as unacceptable. Velleius Paterculus (2.72.3) describes him as *eminentissimae ac nobilissimae simplicitatis vir* but Velleius was writing when Lucius' son Gnaeus was an influential member of the imperial family.

5.1

ex Antonia maiore: she had been born in 39 BC and was the elder daughter of M. Antonius and Caesar's niece Octavia, and so gave the Domitii their earliest connection with the family of the Caesars. Tacitus (*Ann.* 4.44 and 12.64) erroneously calls Nero's grandmother Antonia minor (born 36 BC), confused no doubt because the younger sister was historically the more important as the mother of Germanicus and of the emperor Claudius.

patrem Neronis...in posterum sanxit: little is known of Cn. Domitius Ahenobarbus, consul in 32. He cannot have been a companion of Caius Caesar, grandson of Augustus, who was in the East in 1 BC, as he would have been far too young, perhaps not even born, if he held the consulship at the minimum age for a patrician, which was 32; Velleius Paterculus (2.10.2) calls him *iuvenis* in his historical work completed by 30. Perhaps Domitius was a *comes* of Germanicus Caesar, father of Gaius (Caligula), who was in the East in 17. As in the case of his father, the anecdotes have been chosen for their suitability in foreshadowing Nero. Which of his sisters (6.3 below) made the witticism which has been lost is unknown. *domini factionum*, the businessmen who hired out horses, equipment and professional riders to the magistrates putting on the games. Their relationship with their professionals would obviously have been affected if the appropriate prize money were witheld; see Cameron (1976) 6.

maiestatis quoque...aquae intercutis: the charges against him are also mentioned by Tacitus (*Ann.* 6. 47.2) and Dio (58.27.5) and were made in the first few weeks of 37. On Domitius' sister Lepida, see 6.3 below. Pyrgi (S. Severa) was on the coast of Etruria. Domitius' death was due to dropsy (*aqua intercus*) and took place in late 40 or very early in 41; see 6.3 below.

ex Agrippina Germanico genita: Julia Agrippina (Agrippina the younger) was born on 6 November 15. It was through her that Nero derived his direct descent from Augustus; her mother, wife of Germanicus, was the elder Agrippina, daughter of Augustus' daughter Julia and M. Agrippa. She was married to Domitius in 28; marriage at this young age was common for girls in the imperial family and among the Roman nobility in general. Suetonius deliberately concentrates on the Domitian ancestry of Nero, not the descent from Augustus, though this would have been clear to knowledgeable readers.

6.1

Nero natus est...Kal. Ian: Tiberius died on 16 March 37. Nero's birth on 15 December is confirmed by other sources. The only doubt arises about the year because of inexact statements about his age (e.g. 8 and 57.1 below) but there is no overwhelming reason to reject the date given here; see *PIR* D.127 and Gallivan (1974) 386. There was an imperial property at Antium (Anzio) much favoured by the Julio-Claudians; see e.g. Augustus 58.1; Caligula 8; Tacitus, *Ann.* 15.23.1.

tantum quod...contingeretur: *tantum quod,* 'just as'. *paene ut...contingeretur*, a typical piece of compression; *paene* goes with *priusquam,*'so that he was touched by the sun's rays almost before he was touched by the earth'. The reference is to the custom of laying a newly born child on the ground at the feet of its father for him to acknowledge by picking it up. Dio (61.2.1) has the omen somewhat differently, the light surrounding the infant being supernatural.

de genitura...potuisse: Dio (63.2.3) also has Domitius' remark.

6.2

eiusdem futurae infelicitatis...aulae erat: *eiusdem* refers to Nero, and the *infelicitas* is caused, not suffered by him. *dies lustricus*, the family ceremony which took place on the ninth day after birth at which a boy was formally given his *praenomen*. The right to give the name naturally belonged to the father, but the emperor Gaius (Caligula), Agrippina's brother, along with their uncle Claudius, was asked to the ceremony out of deference. The name he suggested as a joke was presumably Claudius' *praenomen* Tiberius, although a possibility is Claudius' *cognomen* Nero which had been used as a *praenomen* by Gaius' eldest brother, Nero Julius Caesar. In either case the point was that the name was in fact taken by Nero after his adoption by Claudius, which led to his becoming emperor; in 37 he was named Lucius in accordance with the family tradition of the Domitii. There is added irony in the fact that Agrippina, who later engineered

26

the adoption, rejects the omen and cannot take a joke. For the humiliations of Claudius at the court of Gaius, see *Claudius* 8 and 9.

6.3

trimulus patrem...universis bonis: assuming Suetonius is accurate here, Nero's father died after 15 December 40, when Nero would have been three years old, and before January 41 when Gaius was assassinated; so Gallivan (1974) 389. On the importance to the emperor of legacies and the pressures on the wealthy to make bequests to the emperor, see Millar (1977) 153. Gaius had a particularly bad record for seizures of property (*Caligula* 38). For Nero's own record, see 32.2 below.

et subinde matre...nutritus est: Agrippina had been convicted in the autumn of 39 of adultery with M. Aemilius Lepidus, husband of her sister Drusilla (who had died in 38), and of plotting with him against Gaius, for which she was relegated to the Pontian islands (*Caligula* 29.1; Dio, 59.22.6). Nero's aunt Lepida was his father's sister (Domitia) Lepida, the mother of Claudius' wife Messalina (see below). The arrangement cannot have lasted long in view of Agrippina's return from exile as soon as Claudius became emperor.

sub duobus paedagogis saltatore atque tonsore: presumably two slaves or freedmen of Lepida, but the detail looks abusive, since he could hardly have had real *paedagogi* at the age of three. *Paedagogi* of Nero at a later date included the freedman Anicetus (25.2 below and Tacitus, *Ann.* 14.3); Beryllus, a Greek who later held the important post of *ab epistulis* according to Josephus (*A.J.* 20.183); and two respectable philosophers, Alexander of Aegae in Cilicia and Chaeremon of Alexandria.

Crispi Passieni: C. Sallustius Passienus Crispus, grandnephew of the historian Sallust, was a close friend of the emperor Gaius. In 44 he was consul for the second time. He had been husband of Domitius' other sister, normally referred to simply as Domitia to distinguish her from Lepida. The reasons for their divorce and Crispus' marriage to Agrippina early in the principate of Claudius are unknown but his great wealth was perhaps a factor. He was certainly dead by 49 when Agrippina married Claudius; Gallivan (1974) 301 suggests that he died in 44; according to the Scholiast on Juvenal, 4.81, Agrippina poisoned him and his estate amounted to 200 million sesterces.

6.4

Britannici aemulum: Britannicus was the son of Claudius and Messalina.

quasi locates this highly improbable story before the fall of Messalina.

quae fabula exorta est: Tacitus (*Ann.* 11.11.6) is similar and likewise regards it as popular rumour but Dio (61.2.4) has a different notion, that the soothsayers interpreted the serpent's skin as meaning that Nero would receive power from an old man.

7.1

circensibus ludis...lusit: one of the spectacles included in the celebration by Claudius of the Secular Games in 47 was a traditional pageant performed by young boys of noble family on the theme of the Trojan War. A fuller version is given by Tacitus (*Ann.* 11.11.5). It seems that Nero and Britannicus (see below) were the leaders of the opposing sides. The pageant (*lusus Troiae*) had apparently been revived by Augustus (*Augustus* 43) and was traced back by Virgil (*Aeneid* 5.545-603) to the funeral games held by Aeneas for Anchises.

undecimo aetatis...adoptatus est: the date of the adoption was 25 February 50, when he was twelve years and two months old. There is either a manuscript error in Suetonius (Gallivan (1974) 301) or Suetonius has incorrectly transcribed his source. He has omitted to mention specifically the marriage of Agrippina to Claudius which took place in 49 and was the essential preliminary to the adoption of Nero. For the circumstances of the adoption, see Tacitus, *Ann.* 12.25.26, *Claudius* 27.2, and Dio, 60.33.22. Britannicus, son of Claudius and Messalina, was slightly over three years younger than Nero, and the precedent of the adoption by Tiberius of Germanicus, who was two years older than Tiberius' own son Drusus, was quoted. Agrippina's influence was no doubt paramount in the affair and the scandalous behaviour (or treason) of Messalina in 48 could not have helped the younger boy's position.

Annaeoque Senecae...traditus: to Suetonius, Seneca is nothing more than Nero's tutor; see 35.5 and 52 below, where he is called Nero's *praeceptor.* Suetonius thus provides no information on the vexed question of Seneca's part in Nero's govern-ment. Tacitus (*Ann.* 12.8.3) dates the beginning of Seneca's tutorship to 49 when he was recalled through Agrippina's influence from the exile into which he had been sent in 41 by Claudius on a charge of adultery with Agrippina's sister Julia Livilla. The question of his guilt is obscure, as is that of a connection with the charge against Agrippina of adultery with Lepidus (6.3 above). At least the whole affair shows Seneca as a figure in 'court circles' and hence well known to Agrippina towards the end of the reign of Gaius. *iam tunc senatori* is slightly tendentious since Seneca would have obtained senatorial rank when he became *quaestor* some time before 39. His tasks were no doubt primarily to teach Nero the art of rhetoric and to provide him with wordly advice on imperial behaviour; see in general Griffin (1976) *passim*. Seneca's dream is not recorded elsewhere; the C. Caesar mentioned is Caligula.

namque Britannicum...conatus est: Tacitus (*Ann.* 12.41.6-8), dates the incident to 51 after Nero had received the *toga virilis*. In his version it is Agrippina, not Nero, who complains to Claudius, and has Britannicus' tutors removed; see also Dio, 60.32.5. *ex consuetudine*, 'out of habit', but this seems hardly likely; Britannicus would have addressed his brother before the adoption as 'Lucius'. No doubt a quarrel between the boys is at the heart of the story. It may be noted that in Tacitus' version Britannicus calls Nero 'Domitius' and the Elder Pliny on several occasions abusively refers to Nero as Domitius Nero (e.g. *N.H.* 7.45 and 11.238); see also 41.1 below for the edicts of Vindex in the last months of Nero's reign which also used his original name. There was obviously some propaganda value in stressing that Nero was not a true Claudius (nor for that matter a Julius). His name after his adoption was Tiberius Claudius Nero Caesar.

amitam autem...rea premebatur: Tacitus dates the affair to 54 and gives an idiosyncratic account, stressing rivalry between the two for Nero's loyalty, Lepida trying to spoil him and Agrippina to dominate him, but the question of the succession was involved. Whether or not Claudius was reconsidering the precedence accorded to Nero (*Claudius* 43; Dio, 60.34.1; Tacitus, *Ann.* 12.64.3), this remained a possibility especially as Britannicus approached his fourteenth birthday when he might receive the *toga virilis* as Nero had done. Britannicus' chief support was his grandmother Lepida. Tacitus describes her as being not far removed from Agrippina in *forma, aetas, opes*, but he must be wrong about their ages. Agrippina was certainly born in 15, at which date Lepida's mother, the elder Antonia, would have been 54; we must indeed assume that Lepida was many years older than Agrippina. In the same passage Tacitus has also erroneously described her as the daughter of the younger Antonia; the source of his errors is not identifiable. Lepida was accused of attempting to bring about Agrippina's death by magic spells, and of endangering the peace of Italy by not keeping her numerous slaves in Calabria under control, for which she was condemned to death; see Tacitus, *Ann.* 12.64 and 65, who has no word of Nero giving evidence. The trial was probably held by Claudius in person.

7.2

deductus in forum...praetulit: Nero received the *toga virilis* in 51 when he was thirteen, before the usual minimum age which was after the end of a boy's fourteenth year. *tiro*, from the original meaning of a new recruit, here of a first appearance in public as an adult. *donativum*, specifically a money gift to soldiers (no doubt here just the praetorians) as opposed to *congiarium*, money distributed to the people of Rome. *decursio*, a ceremonial parade. On these events, see Tacitus, *Ann.* 12.41.

apud eundem consulem...a Claudio esset: *eundem*, Claudius (*patri* in the previous sentence); the ceremonies had taken place in 51, the year of Claudius' fifth consulship, and Suetonius places the speeches at the same date; Tacitus (*Ann.* 12.58), however, puts them in 53. The *colonia* of Bononia (Bologna) had suffered severe damage from fire and was given 10 million sesterces in aid; Rhodes, whose free status had been abrogated by Claudius because some Roman citizens had been crucified there, now recovered it again, only to lose it permanently under Vespasian; Ilium (Troy), always a privileged city since coming under Roman rule because of the legendary connection between Troy and Rome, received some additional privilege in excess even of the freedom from tribute already granted (*Claudius* 25). Nero, who had had several Greek-speaking teachers, was no doubt already fluent in the language but the speeches were probably written for him as is attested for future occasions (Tacitus, *Ann.* 13.3.3).

Nero's prefecture of the city is not otherwise known, being omitted by Tacitus; it is clearly prior to the marriage to Octavia in 53. It was presumably held for a few days while Claudius was absent from Rome celebrating the *Feriae Latinae* (*sacro Latinarum*) on the Alban Mount.

nec multo post...venationem: Claudia Octavia, Claudius' daughter by Messalina, was born in early 40 or possibly in 39 (Gallivan (1974a) 116-117). She had been betrothed in infancy to a connection of the imperial house, L. Junius Silanus. After his death she was betrothed to Nero in 49; the marriage was in 53. Octavia had formally been adopted into another family since Nero was her brother after his adoption (Dio, 60.33.9). The *circenses* promised for Claudius' recovery from an illness are mentioned in Dio, 60.7.3.

8.1
septemdecim natus...iam vesperi: Claudius died on 13 October 54, so Nero was not seventeen for another two months. Seneca (*Apocolocyntosis* 2) gives the time of Claudius' death as *inter sextam et septimam*, whereas for Suetonius (and for Tacitus, *medio diei*) this is the time for Nero's appearance after Claudius' death. The narratives of Suetonius, Tacitus (*Ann.* 12.69), and Dio (61.3) are very similar; Nero first appears before the guard on duty (*excubitores*, compare Tacitus, *cohortem quae more militiae excubiis adest*); he is then taken to the *castra praetoria*

and after addressing the soldiers (*militibus appellatis*) goes on to the senate house. A donative equivalent to that paid by Claudius was promised to the praetorians. Acclamation by the soldiers before formal bestowal of powers and titles by the Senate was already the standard procedure. Dio says the speeches were composed by Seneca. Nero's dynastic claim to succeed was obvious; besides being the elder son of Claudius, by adoption, he was the heir of Caligula through his mother and a great-great grandson of Augustus. Britannicus' postion, even as the son of Claudius, who was not of the line of Augustus, was much weaker.

ex immensis...propter aetatem: all the powers of the princeps, accumulated over a long period by Augustus, and since added to, especially by Claudius, were now voted en bloc; in spite of Suetonius' *immensis*, there is no reason to suppose that any further additions were now made. Nero refused the title *pater patriae* in 54, but coinage of late 55 or 56 shows that he had adopted it after not much more than a year (*BMC* 1.201).

9.1

orsus hinc...consecravit: Claudius' funeral, followed by his enrollment among the gods (*consecratio*), took place before the end of the year (Tacitus, *Ann.* 13.2.6 and 12.69.4); there was an interval between the funeral and consecration. The model for the lavish funeral was that of Augustus (Dio, 60.35.2; Tacitus, *Ann.* 12.69.4). Gaius had been privately buried and, although Tiberius had a public funeral, it may not have been lavish in view of opinion at the time.

The funeral speech or *laudatio* (*laudavit*) was composed by Seneca and according to Tacitus raised a laugh because of an inappropriate reference to Claudius' *providentia* and *sapientia*. Claudius was the first emperor to be declared a god since Augustus; it was an inevitable result of the influence exercised, for the moment at least, by Agrippina; it would add some prestige to Nero. A priesthood was established, a temple of Claudius begun and Nero was styled *divi Claudi f(ilius)* on coins and inscriptions. However, the temple was left unfinished until the time of Vespasian; that the deification was regarded by some as laughable is shown by Seneca's remarkable satire the *Apocolocyntosis* which was probably circulated as early as 55.

memoriae Domiti...habuit: he received a public statue (Tacitus, *Ann.* 13.10.1) and his birthday was annually celebrated in the prayers of the Arval brethren (Smallwood (1967) nos. 19, 21 and 22).

matri summam...vectus est: presumably an exaggeration, but allegations that Agrippina dominated Nero's government for a while occur in other sources and appear to have some foundation. Dio (61.3.2) has a similar general statement: 'at first Agrippina conducted all the business of government for him', and goes on to mention their use of the same litter. Tacitus (*Ann.* 13.2.5) has the detail of the watchword, but not tied to the day of accession. Dio alleged that she even corresponded with foreign kings and received embassies, which looks like a tendentious version of her attempt, prevented by Seneca, to receive an embassy from Armenia while sitting alongside Nero (Tacitus, *Ann.* 13.5.3). For some months her image on the coins was as prominent as that of Nero (*BMC* 1.200 and 201).

Antium coloniam...sumptuosissimi fecit: curiously misplaced in Suetonius' account of the first weeks of Nero's reign which otherwise proceeds chronologically to the end of the first sentence in 10 below. Suetonius includes honouring his birthplace (Antium) among Nero's displays of *pietas*, a characteristically Roman view. According to Tacitus (*Ann.* 14.27.1) the *colonia* of Antium (Anzio), founded as far back as 338 BC, did not receive its reinforcement of veteran praetorians until 60. It may be that a plan for the settlement, or for the harbour, not mentioned by Tacitus, was first proposed at the beginning of the reign to honour Nero's birthplace. According to Tacitus the settlement of the colonists did not revive the town.

10.1

ex Augusti praescripto imperaturum se professus: following the funeral and consecration of Claudius, Nero delivered before the Senate what is often referred to as his 'programme speech', *formam futuri principatus* as Tacitus calls it in his version (*Ann.* 12.4.2). Very likely the assurance that he would rule *ex Augusti praecepto* occurred in it. According to Tacitus' account, the emphasis was on not following the example of Claudius; he would not take cognizance of all sorts of cases at private trials within the palace; there would be an end to graft; imperial freedmen would not play a part in public policy; the Senate would retain its traditional role in Italy and the (so-called) senatorial provinces. Unfortunately, to claim to follow the example of Augustus was already a commonplace. According to Dio (61.3.1) the speech was written by Seneca, which is likely enough, and was so well received that the senate decreed that it should be inscribed on a silver tablet and read at the start of each year when new consuls entered office.

liberalitatis...clementiae...comitatis: generosity, humanity, affability; these constitute a minor *divisio* (see introduction: Structure of *Nero*). The first two denote approved imperial 'virtues' but *comitas* was slightly different, a point emphasised by *ne...quidem*; none of Nero's predecessors could have laid claim to this character trait. *comitas* was highly esteemed by, for example, Cicero.

Suetonius now departs from his description of Nero's first few weeks as emperor and gives examples of these three qualities which extend over a considerable period of time.

graviora vectigalia...aut minuit: according to Tacitus (*Ann.* 13.50 and 51) in response to complaints about extortion by the *publicani* (the tax collecting companies) Nero suggested in 58 that all *vectigalia*, indirect taxes farmed by the *publicani*, should be abolished; the most important were *portoria*, tolls and dues levied on the movement of goods within the empire. Nero was talked out of this grandiose but impracticable proposal, and contented himself with issuing edicts designed to check extortion by the *publicani*. Some dues were abolished altogether and others on the transport of grain within provinces made easier; presumably Suetonius is referring to these. Since the state's revenues would be diminished, such alleviations could be described as *liberalitas*.

praemia delatorum...redegit: the date of this measure is not known. The *lex Papia Poppaea* of 9 was the final stage of Augustus' social legislation, designed in part to raise the birth rate in Italy. Some provisions in the law laid fiscal penalties on citizens who remained unmarried, and no doubt *delatores*, who made a living by bringing such persons before the courts, were highly unpopular, as was the law itself.

divisis populo...menstruum gratuitum: Nero's *liberalitas* is here exemplified by more traditional examples. The *congiarium* (cash gift) of 400 sesterces per citizen was distributed in 57 (Tacitus, *Ann.* 13.31.2), the largest such distribution since the early years of Augustus. It was celebrated on the coinage of 64 or later and a second *congiarium* of unknown date is also recorded (*BMC* 1.224 and 225).

In 58 (Tacitus, *Ann.* 13.34.1-3) three needy senators were granted an annual income but only one, Valerius Messala, received the enormous figure of half a million sesterces a year; Suetonius' *quibusdam* is one of his generalisations from a particular instance. As early as 15 Tiberius had given a grant to an impoverished senator to save him from falling below the senatorial census (one million sesterces) and thus suffering the disgrace of losing his position in the senate.

The free corn to the praetorians began to be distributed in 65 after the suppression of the Pisonian conspiracy (36.1 below) and was equivalent to a substantial increase in pay since deductions for food were normally made from a soldier's pay.

10.2

et cum de supplicio...nescire litteras: Seneca (*de clementia* 2.1.1) quotes this remark as *vellem nescire litteras*, and says it was made when Burrus was pressing Nero to sign warrants for the execution of two brigands. The *de clementia* was written by Seneca for Nero as a sort of 'Mirror of Princes' as early as 55, and the remark was obviously a good example of *clementia*. Whether Suetonius knew Seneca's work, or whether Nero's remark was more widely known and quoted in one of the historical sources cannot be determined.

ad campestres exercitationes suas admisit et plebem: Suetonius here turns to examples of Nero's *comitas*. The *campestres exercitationes* were the traditional quasi-military exercises performed on the Campus Martius. To invite crowds to watch the emperor perform them was clearly a popular gesture.

declamavitque publice: this must refer not to speeches of a political nature such as the 'programme speech' but to *declamationes*, displays of rhetorical technique which Nero, like all Romans of the upper class, would have learned in schools of rhetoric, or from private tutors. It is difficult to accept that the occasion was truly public; for Augustus listening to a *declamatio* by the young Claudius, see *Claudius* 7. See 52 below for an allegation against Seneca's influence on Nero's reading of earlier orators.

recitavit et carmina...Iovi Capitolino dicata: it is at first sight difficult to relate Suetonius' apparent approval of Nero's recitation of his poetry with his later condemnation of his other artistic pursuits. However, literary accomplishment, even in poetry, was quite acceptable in a member of the Roman upper class and even in the imperial family; the normal method of 'publication' was by a *recitatio* before invited friends (i.e. *domi*). Suetonius does appear also to differentiate Nero's recitation of his own poetry *in theatro*, which appears to be tolerable, from his public stage performances; the event probably took place in his private theatre. See 52.1 below for other evidence of Nero's poetry.

11.1

spectacula plurima et varia genera edidit: the provision of spectacles of various sorts was an obligation amounting to political necessity for the emperors and Suetonius regards their extent and magnificence as worthy of praise in any emperor. For example, the spectacles put on by Augustus are described at length (*Augustus*, 43-45) and introduced by the words *spectaculorum et assiduitate et varietate et magnificentia omnes antecessit* (see also *Claudius* 21). The information included in the various *Lives* probably derived from Suetonius' researches which went into his lost work, the *ludicra historia* (see Introduction).

iuvenales, circenses, scaenicos ludos: another brief *divisio*. The *iuvenales ludi* are named before the traditional types of *ludi* (below) because they were a novelty introduced by Nero, but they were more like the usual *ludi* than the *Neronia* which are discussed in 12.3. Otherwise known as the *Iuvenalia* (Tacitus, *Ann.* 14.15.1), Greek νεανισκεύματα (Dio, 61.19.1), they took place in 59. According to Dio they celebrated the first occasion his beard was shaved, a traditional Roman family occasion. But it appears from Tacitus (*Ann.* 15.33.1) that they were repeated perhaps annually at least until 64. The *circenses ludi* and *scaenici ludi* were the Roman games par exellence, the former being chariot races, the latter theatrical shows of various kinds. Under Augustus there were 77 days of *ludi* of which 17 were *circenses*, 56 *scaenici*, and the remainder ceremonial. The number of *circenses* increased throughout the centuries, the initial disparity being due to the fact that they were much more expensive to put on. Most of the regular *ludi* were put on and paid for by the praetors under regulations established by Augustus, but the emperor sponsored a number himself; see Balsdon (1969) 244ff.

gladiatorum munus: note the correct distinction made by Suetonius; gladiatorial displays were in principle not part of the *ludi*, although the original conception of the *munus*, a sacrifice of blood in honour of the dead, had been largely forgotten, and the displays had become just another form of popular entertainment. All the major gladiatorial exhibitions were given by emperors, and only small ones by the magistrates with few combatants and under strict conditions, for reasons of security.

iuvenalibus senes...ad lusum: Suetonius, like Dio, fails to point out that the *Iuvenalia* took place technically in private, however many guests might be invited. The elderly *consulares* are unknown, but Dio mentions Aelia Catella, an octogenarian of distinguished family, presumably one of the elderly matrons, or the only one, if Suetonius as elsewhere is generalising from the particular. Tacitus (*Ann.* 14.15.2) is heavily rhetorical and just as indefinite about the true facts: *non nobilitas cuiquam, non aetas aut acti honores impedimento quo minus Graeci Latinive histrionis artem exercerent...quin et feminae inlustres deformia meditari.* The *Iuvenalia* appear to have been essentially an elaborate private theatrical show at which Nero himself performed, along with some members of the senatorial class.

35

circensibus loca...tribuit: the allocation of special seats in the Circus to the *equites* took place in 63 (Tacitus, *Ann.* 15.32.2); they had had them in the theatres since 67 BC by virtue of the *lex Roscia*.

11.2

ludis quos pro aeternitate...sustinuerunt: it is not known which *ludi* Nero desired should be called *maximi*; the expression *pro aeternitate imperii* may indicate that they followed his 'escape' from Agrippina's alleged plot (see 34 below). Suetonius' note about the theatrical appearances of senators and knights may also be a clue. According to Tacitus (*Ann.* 14.14.1ff.) after his mother's death, and before the *Iuvenalia*, when Nero took up chariot racing in a semi-private fashion, he also *nobilium posteros egestate venalis in scaenam deduxit*. Dio, in a very rhetorical passage (61.17.2ff.), expatiates on the degradation of descendants of past Roman heroes through their appearances on stage which occurred at games held not long before the *Iuvenalia* 'in honour of his mother'. The final words are erroneous; Dio may have misunderstood his source or the error may be due to the excerptor.

notissimus eques...decucurrit: the elephant story appears in Dio 61.17.2 without mention of the Roman knight. *catadromum*, a Greek formation, is probably a sort of corral of ropes rather than a tightrope.

Afrani togata: Lucius Afranius was born c.150 BC, a generation after Terence. His comedies, all lost, were popular for several centuries. They were *comoediae togatae*, i.e. their subject matter was drawn from the domestic life of Italian towns. It is to be supposed that Nero was present at the performance, which would have been remembered as much for the omen of the title as for the largesse. It is not clear whether this and the next item are to be referred to the *ludi maximi* or not.

sparsa et populo missilia: *missilia* were balls with the names of the prizes written on them; Nero threw them into the crowds who scrambled for them; see also Dio, 61.18.1. Augustus amused himself in this way on a minor scale (*Augustus* 98).

12.1

hos ludos...e proscaeni fastigio: from the top of the *proscaenium*, directly overlooking the stage.

munere quod in amphitheatro...ne noxiorum quidem: it seems that Nero put on only one *munus*. Suetonius does not say that no one was killed, which would be incredible, but that he spared all losers who had not been killed in the fights, even those condemned for criminal offences. Nero's wooden amphitheatre was built, or perhaps completed in 57 (Tacitus, *Ann.* 13.31.1). Pliny (*N.H.* 16.200) mentions a larch beam of record size used in its construction.

exhibuit autem...existimationis integrae: the figures would imply that over half the members of the senate took part; they appear excessive even as a total of all who appeared in the small but regular *munera* put on by others during Nero's principate. Hence Bradley approves Lipsius' emendation to *quadragenos ...sexagenosque.* The glamour which surrounded the profession of gladiator is however notorious and there had always been men of senatorial and equestrian rank to volunteer to fight as gladiators in defiance of social convention and senatorial decrees of Augustan date (*Augustus* 43.3; Dio, 48.43.3 and 56.25.7). Their appearance as *confectores bestiarum* (i.e. *bestiarii*) is more surprising since they did not have the appeal of gladiators (Balsdon (1969) 309). Tacitus is guarded, not mentioning senators and dating to 58 the statement *notos quoque equites Romanos operas arenae promittere subegit donis ingentibus* (*Ann.* 14.14.6). Dio (61.9.1) says that 30 *equites* fought as gladiators, but another allegation (61.17.3) that men *and women* of both orders appeared on the stage, in the circus and in the amphitheatre, looks like a rhetorical combination.

exhibuit et naumachiam: Suetonius here begins to add to the list of *spectacula* outlined at 11.1. The *naumachia*, a sham naval battle, is presumably the one referred to by Dio (62.15.1); after a *venatio*, the amphitheatre was filled with water and the *naumachia* took place. Then it was drained and a gladiatorial show was put on; the date was 64. Claudius had staged a spectacular *naumachia* on the Fucine Lake (*Claudius* 21); see also *Divus Iulius* 39.

pyrrhichas quasdam...singulis optulit: pyrrhic dances were highly traditional exercises performed with weapons in Greek cities and approved of even by Plato. The *ephebi* were Greek youths of 18 to 20 years old. Those who had taken part in a display of pyrrhic dances put on by Julius Caesar were sons of leading men from the cities of Asia and Bithynia, and it is probable that those who performed for Nero were of similar standing; hence the grant of Roman citizenship was not inappropriate; see *Divus Iulius* 39; Pliny *N.H.* 7.204; *PW* IV (A) 2.2240.

12.2

taurus Pasiphaam...cruore respersit: these look like attempts to create spectacularly realistic interludes in tragedies on Greek mythological subjects; for other examples see Cicero, *Ad fam.* 7.1.2 and Horace, *Epistles* 2.1.182-213.

nam perraro...spectare consueverat: Suetonius notes the place from which Nero watched shows in the amphitheatre; see above for his seat in the theatre. The emperor's presence and appropriate demeanour at an increasing number of spectacles at Rome was an essential element in his standing with the masses. Nero clearly began by watching from the imperial box in semi-privacy, but then appeared in full view of all. The podium (*podio*) was the raised platform surrounding the arena.

12.3

instituit et quinquennale...appellavit Neronia: this new festival was introduced in 60. Suetonius uses the official designation; coins were issued with the words *certamen quinquennale*, variously abbreviated (*BMC* 1.250ff.). Tacitus (*Ann.* 14.20.1) calls it *quinquennale ludicrum*. The adjective indicates that the festival was to be celebrated every fifth year, using the Roman tradition of the lustrum, whereas the traditional festivals of the Greek world were celebrated every fourth year; no doubt the difference was to make the innovation more acceptable to Roman opinion. It appears from Suetonius that the popular designation *Neronia* was Nero's own invention. Games of Greek type had in fact been put on at Rome by Augustus in honour of his victory at Actium, but they seem not to have been repeated after his death (unlike the similar games he instituted at Nicopolis). There had also been athletic contests, a characteristically Greek custom. The novelty of Nero's games, stressed also by Tacitus, was their quinquennial repetition and the emphasis laid on music, poetry and declamation. The latter events took place in Nero's new amphitheatre, the athletics in the *Saepta*, an enclosure on the Campus Martius, and the chariot racing in the Circus of Gaius and Nero. Tacitus gives an amusing account of the arguments for and against the new games; a material point was clearly that the cost fell on Nero, not the praetors; see also Dio, 61.21.1 and 2.

dedicatisque thermis...praebuit: the dedication of the gymnasium took place in 61 (Tacitus, *Ann.* 14.47.3) but it is hard to believe that it was not already in use during the *Neronia*. The Latin authors and Dio (61.21.1) all report the dedication and the formal distribution to senators and knights of oil (used by athletes to rub their bodies before the competitions) in almost identical words. The *thermae* are not dated but are associated with the gymnasium and no doubt built at the same time. Martial later wrote (7.34.4-5): *quid Nerone peius? / quid thermis melius Neronianis?*

magistros...praetorum: the appointment of men of consular rank as presidents elevated the *Neronia* above other *ludi*, presided over by praetors.

deinde in orchestram...statuam iussit: in 60 Nero did not compete in person in the contests of rhetoric and Latin poetry (Tacitus, *Ann.* 14.21.5) nor in lyre-playing (Dio, 61.21.2) but merely received the prizes. When the *Neronia* were repeated in 65 the Senate offered him the prizes in advance but by then he was determined to perform himself; see 21 below, Tacitus, *Ann.* 16.4ff., and Dio, 62.29.1.

12.4

ad athletarum...spectare conceditur: Augustus' prohibition against women seeing athletics because the athletes competed naked was evidently still in force, and Nero characteristically justified a change in favour of the Vestals by a Greek precedent. In the theatre and amphitheatre Vestals had reserved places in prominent positions.

13.1

non immerito...rettulerim: Suetonius considers that the reception of Tiridates, king of Armenia, was a *spectaculum* of a very special kind; it seems that it was the most lavish reception given to any foreign ruler (and indeed a client king at that) up to Suetonius' time. It is however interesting in this passage that he concentrates on the historical importance of the king's visit which was his formal investiture as king of Armenia, and on the military ceremonial in which Nero appeared as a *triumphator*. Dio (63.1-7) also has an unusually favourable, even enthusiastic, description of the event, with some close verbal similarities to Suetonius. He has further interesting detail on the protocol including the actual words of submission by Tiridates and of the investiture by Nero. Furthermore, whereas Dio notes without comment that the cost of the visit was 800,000 sesterces per day for nine months, Suetonius has singled out this detail, which he calls scarcely credible, for criticism as an example of Nero's *luxuria* (30.2 below). The Elder Pliny has some unenthusiastic references to the cost (*N.H.* 30.16 and 33. 54) but this does not mean he was not a source for the information in Suetonius and Dio.

Trouble between Rome and Parthia over the question of paramountcy in Armenia had a long history; for much, though not all, of the period from Augustus onwards Rome had had the advantage, but in the last years of Claudius, Vologaeses, king of Parthia, had installed his brother Tiridates as king of Armenia. This would have bound Armenia closely to Parthia and in 54 Nero's government sent the general Domitius Corbulo with reinforcements to the East to try to regain control of the disputed kingdom. For some eight years, in a series of complicated military and diplomatic manoeuvres, the two imperial powers contended with each other, never quite coming into an all-out open conflict which both were determined to avoid if at all possible. In 62, when Corbulo was replaced, Roman arms suffered a humiliating setback at Rhandeia in Armenia (see note on 39.1 below) but in 63 Corbulo returned with even larger forces and obliged Tiridates to agree, without a battle, to a compromise; Rome would agree to recognize him as king of Armenia provided that he received the insignia from Nero at Rome. This compromise had been suggested several years before; it represented a diminution of Rome's position in Armenia in real terms, though it may be noted that the solution is not criticised by any of the sources. It continued for many decades in spite of occasional breaches, for example by the Parthians in the time of Trajan; see also Warmington (1969) 85-100.

13.2

tiara: a turban or something similar.

diadema: a symbol of royalty, originally Persian, adopted by Alexander and his successors, and subsequently worn by emperors on Roman imperial coinage.

imperator consalutatus: confirmed by the coinage (*BMC* 1.clxviff.).

Ianum geminum clausit...bello: the rarely used ceremony indicating general peace on land and sea. The monument of Ianus Geminus, apparently in the form of an arched gate, stood in the Forum. The coins bear the legend *Pace P.R. Terra Mariq. Parta Ianum Clusit* (or minor variations); the earliest appear to date from 64, so the ceremony may have been repeated in 66 (*BMC* 1. clxxiv). *tamquam* expresses a real, not supposed reason.

14.1

consulatus quattuor gessit: in 55, 57, 58 and 60. Contrary to what Suetonius says, Nero held the consulship of 57 for the whole year (*CIL* IV.3340). Suetonius ignores the sole consulship which Nero assumed in the last few weeks of his life (see 43.2 below). However, years in which he did not serve the full term allowed others to serve as suffect consuls – there were always those entitled to such rewards. Suetonius' readers might compare Nero favourably in this matter with Domitian who held ten consulships during his principate, seven in successive years.

15.1

in iuris dictione...pronuntiabat: an emperor had to deal personally, and normally in public, with much legal business, not all of it important, and the way in which he handled it was important to his reputation. Claudius was thought to be over-zealous and unpredictable. Nero's methods as described here are unexceptionable; to postpone judgement for a day was approved practice. The point-by-point procedure would tend to cut out unnecessary speeches by advocates and is found under Trajan (Pliny, *Epistles* 6.22.2). Both Augustus and Claudius had from time to time taken written opinions from their *amici*, who sat with them, though the emperor, like any magistrate, had sole responsibility whatever the opinions of his *amici*. Hence Suetonius is tendentious in his implication, though such an allegation could always be made; see Millar (1977) 228ff.

15.2

in curiam...admisit: traditional social prejudice dictates Suetonius' approach. Claudius had proclaimed that he would not give senatorial rank except to a man whose father and grandfather were both free born, but had nevertheless given it to the son of a freedman (*Claudius* 24.1). Nero for some time (*diu*) at least did not give the rank to the son of a freedman. Presumably this was one of the policies of his earlier years when the memory of Claudius' powerful freedmen was still vivid.

honores denegavit: not excluded from the Senate but prevented from holding further office. Perhaps this is generalising from the individual given senatorial rank by Claudius.

candidatos...praeposuit: this happened in 60. The magistrates had been in effect chosen by the Senate since the early days of Tiberius' principate, though the formality of a vote in the *comitia centuriata* survived. On this occasion there were fifteen candidates for the twelve praetorships and the implication of the incident is that normally the numbers of candidates and vacancies was the same. Command of a legion could be held before or after a praetorship and presumably those disappointed in 60 held the magistracy subsequently; see also Tacitus, *Ann.* 14.28.

defunctoque circa...uno die consulis: the date is not known. C. Caninius Rebilus was made consul for one day in 45 BC by Julius Caesar, one of the most notorious examples of his contempt for the political conventions; see Cicero, *ad Fam.* 7.30.

triumphalia ornamenta...causa militari: after the suppression of the Pisonian conspiracy of 65 (see 36 below) Nero awarded honorary triumphs to three men who had particularly helped him; this is presumably the non-military occasion to which Suetonius refers and it is notable that Suetonius does not appear to regard it as in any way reprehensible. The three men were Petronius Turpilianus, consul in 61; M. Cocceius Nerva, the future emperor, who was *praetor designatus* in 65 and hence of quaestorian rank; and the praetorian prefect Tigellinus, an *eques*. Tacitus (*Ann.* 15.72.2), like Suetonius, does not condemn the awards; perhaps even under Hadrian it would have been inappropriate to criticise Nerva. *nonnullis* is another example of Suetonius generalising from a single instance. It may also be noted that, as in a number of items mentioned in 15-17, he has separated facts from their contexts.

de quibusdam rebus...recitabat: consuls had a quaestor especially attached to them as assistant. Perhaps when Augustus ceased to hold the consulship regularly, the emperor was allotted a quaestor, subsequently called the *quaestor Augusti* and later there were two (out of the 20 quaestors each year). Their chief function, as the passage indicates, was to read messages from the emperor to the senate (Ulpian, *Digest* 1.13.1.4). Tacitus (*Ann.* 16.27.2) shows a quaestor reading a message from Nero; Suetonius is referring to an occasion (or occasions) of which we know nothing.

16.1
formam aedificiorum...sumptu suo extruxit: Suetonius ignores the context, namely Nero's regulations for the rebuilding of Rome after the fire of 64, which are described in greater detail but similar words in Tacitus, *Ann.* 15.43.1ff. The streets were to be wider, a maximum height for buildings was prescribed, and the *insulae* (apartment blocks) and *domus* (individual residences) were to have colonnades as an extra precaution against fire, and it was this part of the additional expense of rebuilding which Nero would pay for.

destinarat etiam...urbi inducere: no other source refers to this plan. The pluperfect *destinarat* and *veteri urbi* indicate that it antedated the fire. It is presumably to be associated with the plan to build a canal from Lake Avernus to Ostia, which Suetonius (31 below) regarded as an extravagance. A canal from Ostia to the city would have cut out the difficulties of shipping on the Tiber. The idea of extending the walls of Rome to include Ostia was no doubt based on the Long Walls of Athens. It is curious that Tacitus (*Ann.* 15.43.4) following the passage which has such verbal similarity with the preceding sentence in Suetonius, also mentions Ostia; he says that the marshes there were to be the dumping ground for rubble from the city, to be carried downstream by the corn ships on their return journeys. Perhaps both items were in their common source. Wherever Suetonius got his story it appears to be the only building project of Nero of which he specifically approved; normally he gives credit to emperors for their public works (e.g. *Augustus* 29; *Claudius* 20; *Vespasian* 9) but tends to regard Nero's as extravagance or, as in the case of his amphitheatre and baths, worthy of mention only in passing; see Warmington (1969) 127f.

16.2

multa sub eo...instituta: Suetonius here and in 17 lists a number of 'police measures' and new regulations (*instituta*). The words *sub eo* and the use of the passive voice throughout are presumably meant to indicate that in Suetonius' view Nero was not specifically the initiator but the implication is that they are nevertheless something to put on the credit side of his generally deplored principate. The measures listed are primarily concerned with the city of Rome.

adhibitus sumptibus modus: nothing is known of a *lex sumptuaria* of Nero; perhaps there was an attempt to reinforce the famous laws of Augustus of 22 BC designed to fix maximum expenditure on meals. They were as notoriously ineffective as similar laws in the Republic, as Tiberius pointed out (Tacitus, *Ann.* 3.52-55), but conventional wisdom approved of them.

publicae cenae...sportulae redactae: perhaps associated with the foregoing, which would have covered only private dinner parties. The idea was to prevent wealthy *patroni* from competing in extravagance towards their clients by giving lavish banquets instead of daily food rations (*sportulae*).

interdictum...proponeretur: in contrast with the above two measures which, if observed, would have affected only the rich, this measure affected the poor who were the chief patrons of the *popinae*, establishments where both cooked food and drink could be obtained. The authorities at Rome were always anxious about their popularity (over 100 have been identified at Pompeii alone) and possible effects on public order. Compare the concern with the control and licensing of inns and public houses in England ever since the sixteenth century. Nero's regulation seems designed to diminish the attractiveness of the food sold, in order to lessen the amount of time patrons might spend on the premises. For an earlier proposed restriction, see *Tiberius* 34. Dio (62.14.2) gives Nero's regulation in almost identical words with the comment, 'although he spent practically his whole existence amid tavern life'.

affecti...maleficae: for the reading *affecti* (as opposed to *afflicti*), see K.R. Bradley, *Classical Philology* 22 (1972) 9f. For obvious reasons this passage is often referred to, though it adds nothing to help elucidate the much more famous passage in Tacitus, *Ann.* 15.44.3-8. It should be said that for the suggestion, made from time to time, that the passage is an interpolation, not a shred of evidence exists.

43

superstitionis novae ac maleficae: Tacitus calls Christianity a *superstitio exitiabilis* and the Younger Pliny, contemporary with both Suetonius and Tacitus, a *superstitio prava atque immodica*. Any foreign, but not Greek, religion was liable to be called *superstitio*; Suetonius uses it of the cult of Isis (*Domitian* 1.2; *Claudius* 36.1; and 56 below). There was a long history of attempts at Rome to control the growth of such cults in the city. Suetonius says of Tiberius *externas caerimonias, Aegyptios Iudaicosque ritus compescit* (*Tiberius* 36) and with reference to the same measures Josephus (*A.J.* 18.4) relates that the image of Isis was thrown into the Tiber and her priests crucified. Suetonius clearly approved of such actions, as he did of Claudius' actions against the Druids in Gaul (*Claudius* 25). A notable point is that the repression of the Christians is dissociated from the aftermath of the fire of Rome by Suetonius, whereas for Tacitus, although he has called the new religion an *exitiabilis superstitio*, the punishment of its followers as scapegoats for the fire is another of Nero's crimes. In spite of his manifest desire to have it both ways, the authority of Tacitus is such that there have been few to reject his version, though the difficulties are numerous (for a short account, see Warmington (1969) 125-127); the chief one is that no Christian writer in the next three centuries knows of Nero using the Christians in this way though they knew vaguely of Nero as a persecutor and would have had every incentive to emphasise such an action by a universally condemned ruler. On the other hand, Suetonius has separated several other items from their contexts but it must remain a possibility that he reproduces material indicating that the Christians were attacked as a *superstitio malefica* for strictly traditional religious reasons and that Tacitus has artfully confused the issue by introducing the notion of scapegoats in order to bring yet another charge against Nero.

vetiti quadrigariorum lusus...erat: the popularity of charioteers among all ranks of Roman society was a phenomenon which lasted for many centuries, in spite of the fact that many began life as slaves. The *inveterata licentia* indicates that their freedom from conventional restraints was already long established; see Balsdon (1969) 321ff.

pantomimorum factiones...relegatae: Suetonius has separated an action of which he approved from an anecdote to Nero's discredit (26.2 below). The passages combined are almost identical with Tacitus, *Ann.* 13.25.4, except that Suetonius alleges Nero's personal participation in the riots; see also Dio, 61.8.2. Theatre audiences were notoriously turbulent, and the fans of the pantomime dancers were among the most unrestrained. Tiberius had banished both dancers and the leaders of the fans from Italy (*Tiberius* 37.2). They were readmitted by Gaius. Nero withdrew in 54 the praetorian cohort, which had been necessary to ensure order in the theatres, and riots increased until (in 56) he had to take the same action as Tiberius. They were allowed back some time before 60 (Tacitus, *Ann.* 14.21.7).

17.1

adversus falsarios...ascriberet: also referred to by Dio, 61.7.6; the rule appears to have been introduced in 55.

item ut litigatores...aerario gratuita: the first act of Nero's principate noted by Tacitus (*Ann.* 13.5.1) was a decree of the Senate *ne quis ad causam orandam mercede aut donis emeretur*. The relationship of the decree to what Suetonius says is uncertain. He may refer to a later measure; but Tacitus seems to have in mind bargaining with an advocate for a fee before the case came on, and that the payment of a *certa iustaque merces* (or a *donum*) after the case was permitted. Pliny the Younger (*Epistles*, 5.9.4) refers to such a rule.

utque rerum actu...ad senatum fierent: not known from any other source. The *aerarium* under Augustus had been headed by two praetorian *praefecti*; Claudius appointed quaestors; but in 56 Nero went back to men of praetorian rank (Tacitus, *Ann.* 13.28-29). Apparently they normally had jurisdiction over cases involving debts to the treasury. A transfer of this jurisdiction to *reciperatores* (panels of three or five judges) might seem more impartial, but the change did not last long since the officials of the *aerarium* had jurisdiction again under Domitian. Nero's reform presumably came early in his principate. See Millar (1964) 33-41.

18.1

augendi propagandique...destitit: this has been seen as an oblique criticism of Hadrian's foreign policy (Syme (1958) 490; Townend (1959) 292). But apart from the fact that it occurs among actions of Nero which Suetonius considered unexceptionable, Suetonius has something similar to say of Augustus himself (*Augustus* 21): *tantumque afuit a cupidiate quoquo modo imperium vel bellicam gloriam augendi*; this could be taken (if one assumes a covert reference to Hadrian) as an indication that Suetonius rather approved of a non-expansive policy. The fact is that there are serious problems of method involved in trying to identify hidden references to contemporary events in Roman authors describing past times. On this complex subject, see especially Wallace-Hadrill (1983) 198 ff. However, it can be taken as certain that Suetonius did not believe that it was an obligation on emperors to advance the imperial frontiers, and elsewhere he describes their foreign policies (if such they could be called, often involving no more than the reduction to provincial status of the few remaining small client states) in terms very similar to those he uses of Nero (*Tiberius* 37; *Caligula* 43;

Claudius 17; *Vespasian* 8; *Domitian* 6).

Various theories have been advanced about the proposed withdrawal from Britain, but there seems no reason to doubt the most obvious hypothesis, that it was a short-lived over-reaction to news of the revolt of Boudicca, which at first, with all the legions cut off from their main base (London) must have seemed very serious; nor should the motive for reversing the plan be altogether discounted since Claudius had made a great deal of propaganda about the conquest of Britain and Nero's prestige would have suffered severely if he had withdrawn without a struggle. See Warmington (1976) 42-52.

Ponti modo...concedente Polemone: a small client kingdom along the southern coast of the Black Sea including the old Greek colony of Trapezus (Trebizond). Its king Polemo also ruled part of Cilicia and was given a small part of Armenia in 60. The provincialisation has been dated, on coin evidence (Magie (1950) 1417) to 64 when Pontus was joined to Cappadocia.

item Alpium...formam redegit: almost all the Alpine regions had been provincialised by Augustus but a small area in the region of Mt. Genèvre was left to Julius Cottius, son of a former chieftain, who received Roman citizenship and the title *praefectus civitatium*. The death of his son occurred in 65 and the new province was known as *Alpes Cottiae*.

19.1
peregrinationes: tours outside Italy of a non-military character.

Alexandrina...non posset: the project was planned for 64 (before the fire) and was to be the high point of a tour including other eastern provinces (Tacitus, *Ann.* 15.36.3). Tacitus does not describe the omens in the temple of Vesta, saying merely that Nero had a sudden trembling fit: *seu numine exterrente seu facinorum recordatione.* No emperor had previously visited Alexandria, though Nero's grandfather Germanicus had done so; see also 35.5 below.

19.2
in Achaia...extulit: Suetonius here mentions a relatively creditable action during Nero's famous tour of Greece which began in 66. The tour had in fact originally been thought of in 64, if not 63, but was put off for reasons unknown in favour of the plan to visit the eastern provinces and Alexandria (Tacitus, *Ann.* 15.36.1). When the eastern trip in turn was cancelled Nero returned to his earlier project. The beginning of the canal was in 67. That Nero dug the first sod is confirmed by Dio (63.16) who says that his action stimulated others who had been frightened

by bad omens. Compare the similarly royal ceremonial in which Vespasian began
the work of clearing away the debris from the Capitol (destroyed in 69) by carry-
ing away rubble on his shoulders (*Vespasian* 8). Dio does not criticise the project
and it was generally popular in the Greek world; pseudo-Lucian (*Nero* 1) says
the emperor showed a spirit 'even better than Greek' (see also Philostratus, *Apoll.
Tyan.* 4.24). There had been earlier plans for a canal by Demetrius, Julius Caesar
and Gaius. According to Josephus (*B.J.* 3.10.10) ten thousand captives taken in the
Jewish war were used. The work stopped on Nero's death and was never resumed.
See Warmington (1969) 133.

parabat et ad Caspias...appelabat: this project was apparently one of some importance. The 'Caspian Gates' was the name generally given to the Daryal Gorge,
the chief pass through the central part of the Caucasus; it was in the territory of
the Iberi who were normally clients of Rome and who had played some part in the
campaigns of Corbulo in Armenia. Roman access to the Iberi was up the valley
of the Phasis. The importance of the Caspian Gates was enhanced in the middle of
the first century by the arrival in the steppes north of the Caucasus of formidable
nomads, the Alani, who had already raided south of the mountains in 35. The
expedition was also to include a campaign against the Albani (Tacitus, *Hist.* 1.6),
whose territory was to the east of the Iberi and extended to the Caspian Sea thus
including the Pass of Derbend, a defile between the eastern end of the Caucasus
and the shore of the Caspian. Their status as clients of Rome was at best tenuous.
Nero's plan was thus to establish firm Roman control of both the main passes
through the Caucasus. There had been a reconnaissance of the region during
Corbulo's campaigns and a map had been sent to Rome (Dio, 63.8.2; Pliny, *N.H.*
6.40). According to Pliny the designation 'Caspian Gates' was wrong; it should
have been Caucasian Gates, since the Caspian Gates, famous in the story of
Alexander the Great, were quite different (Sandford (1937) 75ff). It is just possible
that Corbulo's map used the words, quite reasonably, of the Pass of Derbend; for
this was the designation in Byzantine times. It may be that Nero should be
numbered among those Romans who dreamed of imitating Alexander but, in
view of his general lack of interest in military affairs, the remark quoted by
Suetonius could have been a joke. The new legion was the *Legio I Italica*. The
Legio XIV Gemina probably left Britain to join the expedition in 67 and detachments from other legions in Britain, Germany and Illyricum had already arrived
in Egypt in 66 (Josephus, *B.J.* 2.18.8; Tacitus, *Hist.* 1.6.31 and 70). In 75 the
Parthians made a unique proposal to Vespasian that the two empires should
jointly defend the Caucasus. Vespasian rejected this, but appears to have
established firmer Roman control in Iberia (*ILS* 8795; *AE* (1951) 263).

19.3

haec partim...dehinc dicam: the basic *divisio* (see Introduction: Structure of *Nero*). It goes without saying that the sections on *probra* and *scelera* occupy far more space than the preceding relatively favourable aspects of Nero's reign. The sections on *probra*, actions short of actual crimes, are revealing of the attitude of Suetonius and presumably many of his generation towards Nero's commitment to his musical and theatrical interests, and his manifest philhellenism. It is, however, arguable that he found these slightly less distasteful than did Tacitus. The limits of Roman acculturation to Greek civilisation were always flexible. See Wallace-Hadrill (1983) *passim*.

20.1

inter ceteras disciplinas...nullum esse respectum: there is no reason to doubt that Nero took himself extremely seriously as a performer and was prepared to practice hard (see 25.3 and 41 below; Dio, 61.20.2). Dio calls his voice βραχὺ καὶ μέλαν which presumably represents the same source as *exigua et fusca*. In fact, according to Quintilian (11.3.171) the *vox fusca* was the most suitable for conveying emotional, pitiful or dramatic situations, which were precisely those which Nero loved to perform. Dio jeers that he moved his audience to laughter and tears at the same time; if this really happened it might be to Nero's credit as a performer. Balsdon (1969) 287 points out that, whereas we know the names of many famous actors and pantomime dancers from antiquity, Nero is the only outstanding Roman musician known by name. His speciality was to perform not just as a singer or instrumentalist but in the more exacting role of a *citharoedus* who sang to his own accompaniment on the *cithara* in tragic monologues, wearing mask and theatrical costume. See Charlesworth (1950).

20.2

et prodit Neapoli...absolveret nomon: the preceding sentences indicated that his desire to appear on the public stage grew with time. In fact his public debut was as late as 64; previously he had confined himself to performances in a private theatre in his gardens across the Tiber (Tacitus, *Ann.* 14.15.1 and 15.33.1; Pliny, *N.H.* 37.19). The choice of Naples was determined by its Greek character, and his appearance was to be a prelude to his visit to Greece, not yet postponed. In a different version of Nero's apparent danger, Tacitus (*Ann.* 15.33.1ff.) says that the theatre suddenly collapsed after everyone had left.

20.3

captus autem...Alexandri evocavit: the grain fleet from Alexandria always docked at Puteoli. The Alexandrian enthusiasts in the audience were presumably sailors from the fleet.

neque eo segnius...sestertia merebant: an organised claque of *equites Romani* to applaud Nero had been formed in 59 for the *Iuvenalia* (Tacitus, *Ann,* 14.15.8 and 9); its enlargement to a total of 5,000 ordinary citizens no doubt dates from Nero's appearance in public, as Suetonius implies. Dio (61.20.3-4) is anachronistic in dating the enlarged claque to 59 and wrong in saying they were soldiers, though on later occasions soldiers were indeed employed in order to keep the spectators applauding (Tacitus, *Ann.* 16.5.1). Organised rhythmic applause and the chanting of slogans was an established custom in the theatre in late imperial times; see Cameron (1976) 234ff.

21.1

cum magni aestimaret...amicorum intimi: there is an apparent difficulty in Suetonius' statement that the second *Neronia* were held before the due date since Tacitus (*Ann.* 16.4-5) explicitly puts the repetition in 65 which would be correct. However, Suetonius' chronology does not state that the repetition is in the same year (64) as the appearance at Naples, and the anticipation of the date may have been short. There is enough similarity in the descriptions to indicate that the two authors are describing the same event; for an opposite view, see Gallivan (1974) 307. At first Nero contented himself with reciting one of his own poems, *recitatio* of a Latin composition being perhaps tolerable (see 10.2 above); when the public demand for him to display his other talents became persistent, he said at first that he would perform in his private gardens but was, according to Tacitus, prevailed upon to return to the theatre to do so. The future emperor Vitellius, who was presiding over the festival, took the lead in persuading him (*Vitellius,* 4). Nero then formally ordered his name to be added to the list of competitors for the prize for *citharoedi. caelestis vox* appears to have been the prescribed term for Nero's voice; see also Dio, 62.26.3.

21.2

Niobam: for Nero's repertoire, see 21.3 below.

Cluvium Rufum: Cluvius Rufus was consul before 65; as this reference (and other information) indicates he was in Nero's entourage from about that date, specifically involved in his theatrical activities. He supported Galba, Otho and Vitellius in turn in 69 and survived the Flavian victory. In view of his close familiarity with Nero, at least in the second part of his reign, some have seen his historical work as a major source, but little is known of it. See Warmington (1969) 5-7.

dubitavit etiam...decies offerente: the incident is referred to, it seems, by Dio (63.21.2) who names the man concerned, but without giving his rank, as a certain Larcius from Lydia; Dio goes on to say that Nero did perform but refused to accept the money, to preserve his amateur status, as it were, but that Tigellinus the praetorian prefect extorted it anyway.

21.3

tragoedias quoque...opis gratia: Dio (63.9.4-6), in a particularly abusive and rhetorical passage referring to Nero's performances in his tour of Greece, confirms Orestes, Oedipus and Heracles and adds Thyestes and Alcmaeon. The performances were not in tragedies by classic authors or later imitators, but dramatic solos. Dio says that the female masks were all like Poppaea even though she was now dead. The joke about the soldier running to help him also occurs, though it is misunderstood by Dio's excerptor (63.10.2). All Suetonius' examples (including Niobe grieving for her murdered children) involved extremes of emotion and probably appealed to the tastes of many besides Nero and for that matter probably Seneca. His readers might be expected to see or imagine connections between the incest motif in Canace and Oedipus with the allegations about Nero and Agrippina.

22.1

equorum studio...flagravit: Tacitus, *Ann.* 13.3.7 is similar.

prasini agitatorem...ementitus est: the famous four 'factions' – Blues, Greens, Reds and Whites – of the Roman circus had apparently existed from time immemorial, but the predominance of the Blues and Greens was already established in the first century. Fanatical partisanship ran through all classes. Gaius and Domitian, as well as Nero, supported the Greens, Vitellius the Blues. At some date after 65 Nero had the floor of the amphitheatre spread with *chrysocolla* to give it a green appearance and himself performed wearing the colour (Pliny, *N.H.* 30.90). See Cameron (1976) 45ff.

22.2

ne dominis quidem...greges ducere: for the *domini factionum*, see 5 above. It was not worth their while to hire out the horses and equipment for shows lasting less than a full day, but this made it too expensive for the praetors putting on the races. In 54, when the increase in the number of races took place, the praetor Aulus Fabricius Veiento threatened to run dogs instead of horses, but the Blue and Green *domini* still refused to let out their teams; Nero then agreed to pay the prizes himself (Dio, 61.6.1-3).

mox et ipse...magistratus solent: Nero's first appearance as a charioteer *in hortis* was in 59 (Tacitus, *Ann.* 14.14.4) after the death of Agrippina. The emperor's private circus in the imperial gardens in the Vatican valley had been built, or begun, by Gaius and was generally called the Circus of Gaius and Nero. That ordinary Romans were invited in to watch is also asserted by Tacitus. The date of Nero's appearance in the Circus Maximus in unknown but, on the analogy of his first truly public theatrical performance, was not until 65 and may indeed be as late as 66, since it is not in the extant portion of Tacitus' *Annals*.

22.3

Achaiam...petit: the visit to Greece, first projected in 64 (see 19 above) took place in 66, Nero setting out on 25 September of that year (Smallwood (1967) no.25).

instituerant...dignos ait: the implication is that the prizes were sent to him in advance.

Cassiope: a harbour on Corcyra (Corfu). The temple of Jupiter Cassius (Ζεὺς Κάσιος) was well known and mentioned by Pliny, *N.H.* 4.52. The cult derived its name from a hill on the Orontes in Syria, *PW* X (A) 320-321.

23.1

nam et quae diversissimorum...quibusdam iteratis: for the dates, see Gallivan (1974) 307. The list is as follows:

	Last held	Due
Olympic	65	69
Pythian	63	67
Nemean	66	68
Isthmian	65	67

The Pythian and Isthmian games were therefore held in the correct year, the repeated festivals being the Olympic and Nemean.

cum praesentia eius...admoneretur: this must refer to the period towards the end of 67 when disaffection in Rome and the West became serious. Helius was a former freedman of Claudius; as procurator of imperial property in Asia in 54, he had assisted Agrippina in the murder of Junius Silanus in that year (Tacitus, *Ann.* 13.1). His subsequent career is unknown until 67 when he was left to look after affairs in Rome with very great (though presumably unofficial) powers which he is said to have misused (Dio, 64.12.1ff.). He was put to death by Galba.

23.2

cantante eo...funere elati: the story that no one was allowed to leave the theatre (or even the town, if we are to believe Suetonius) while Nero was performing, though probably true enough, was an obvious target for satire. Tacitus (*Ann.* 16.5), perhaps anachronistically, described the rule as applying at the repetition of the Neronia in 65 and alleges that people actually did die during the performances. Dio (63.15.3) has almost the same wording as Suetonius about people pretending to be dead, apparently in reference to the Greek tour. There was a story that the future emperor Vespasian narrowly escaped death because he fell asleep during a performance by Nero (*Vespasian* 4 and Dio, 66.11.2., both set in Greece; Tacitus, *Ann.*.16.5, set in Rome).

adversarios...solebat: very similar in Dio, 63.9.2.

24.1

in certando...detergeret: so Tacitus, *Ann.* 16.4.2.

victorem ipse...pronuntiabat: Dio (63.14.4) does not say that Nero read the announcements personally but gives the actual words: 'Nero Caesar wins this contest and crowns the Roman People and his own universe'.

ac ne cuius...imperavit: this no doubt scurrilous accusation perhaps had its basis in the fact that Nero did remove a number of statues from Greece for the adornment of the Golden House.

24.2

aurigavit...reprehendisset: for his fall, see Dio, 63.14.1.

decedens deinde...pronuntiavit: The proclamation of freedom for the province of Achaia took place on 28 November 67; Gallivan (1974) 308. The text of Nero's brief but grandiloquent speech survives (Smallwood (1967) no.64). The material benefit to the inhabitants was freedom from tribute, only implied by Suetonius' *libertas* but specifically mentioned in Nero's speech. The gesture was unquestionably an aspect of Nero's philhellenism, and the place for the announcement was no doubt chosen because of the proclamation there (in 196 BC by Flamininus) of Roman withdrawal from Greece after the Macedonian War. It was favourably mentioned by Greek intellectuals such as Plutarch, Pausanias and Philostratus as something to put in the balance to Nero's credit. Suetonius is not verbally hostile but perhaps his inclusion of it among the *probra* of Nero indicates that his Flavian sources disapproved, as was to be expected since Vespasian cancelled the grant (*Vespasian* 8). See Warmington (1969) 118. Sections 22-24, like 40-49, show how effective Suetonius could be in a dramatic accumulation of small details. Nero's tour of Greece lent itself to a narrative of a sensational kind by unsympathetic authors, though the contemporary Greek view appears to have been somewhat different. It is unfortunate that we can only surmise what Tacitus made of it.

25.1

reversus e Graecia...Apollinem petit: probably soon after the proclamation at the Isthmus, since he had travelled from Naples to Rome and back again to Naples by the second half of March 68 (see 40.1 below). His freedman Helius had become so alarmed because Nero ignored his reports of disaffection that he went to Greece in person and got him to return to Italy, in spite of the fact that it was now probably mid-winter during which sailing was normally avoided (Dio, 63.19ff.).

The 'triumph' of Nero is described in similar detail and at greater length in Dio, 63.20.1ff. The whole affair was elaborately organised and perhaps Nero's return was not quite so hurried as Dio implies. His ceremonial procession to the Capitol as victor in the Greek games was, if Suetonius and Dio are to be believed, almost a parody of the traditional Roman triumph of a general victorious over foreign enemies, or at any rate it was capable of being so represented. It was natural that the procession should end not at the temple of Jupiter Optimus Maximus but at that of Apollo as patron of the arts. Nero was hailed as 'new Apollo' at Athens (Smallwood (1967) no.145) and Dio says that the slogans shouted by the whole population of Rome were 'Hail Pythian Victor, Augustus, Augustus! Hail to Nero Hercules! Hail to Nero Apollo!'.

25.2

citharoedico habitu...nummum percussit: the issue was apparently made in 64-66, before the tour of Greece. The obverse has the head of Nero, the reverse has Apollo Citharoedus, obviously identified with the emperor (Smallwood (1967) no.144; *BMC* 1.245-246, 250 and 274).

26.1

Sections 26-38 cover the *scelera* of Nero mentioned in the *divisio* (19 above), each of the five main varieties of 'crime' being illustrated by anecdotes.

petulantia: irresponsibility, almost hooliganism.

post crepusculum...ad necem caesus: these activities took place early during Nero's principate and are dated to 56 by Tacitus, *Ann.* 13.25.1-3 and Dio, 61.9.2-3.

The senator mentioned was a young man named Julius Montanus who was forced to commit suicide when he asked for pardon after discovering who it was he had injured; Nero was still behaving this way in 58 (Tacitus, *Ann.* 13.47.2).

26.2

delatus in theatrum...caput consauciavit: see 16.2 where Suetonius separates the reasonable police measure from a discreditable anecdote, whereas Tacitus (*Ann.* 13.25.4) runs them together.

27.2

epulas a medio die...ut appelleret: Tacitus (*Ann.* 14.2.1) refers to Nero feasting at midday in 59; the normal time of the *cena* was, at this period, early in the evening. The public banquet in the *Naumachia*, the artificial lake on which Augustus had staged his mock sea battle, is apparently referred to by Dio (61.20.5) as taking place in 59.

Baiae on the Bay of Naples had long been a favourite resort of wealthy Romans and Nero had a villa there. The descriptions of the taverns and brothels set up along the shore is similar to that given by both Tacitus (*Ann.* 15.37) and Dio (62.15) of a particularly notable boating party given for Nero by Tigellinus in 64, shortly before the fire of Rome. It may be noted that Tacitus claims to describe it in detail (*ut exemplum referam ne saepius eadem prodigentia narranda sit*), while Suetonius, by his use of a succession of imperfects, also conveys the idea that this sort of thing was Nero's habitual conduct.

27.3

indicabat et familiaribus...aliquanto rosaria: Nero used to invite himself to dinner at his friends' homes.

constitit: 'cost'. *mitellita* is obscure, since it only occurs in this passage; it should be an adjective parallel with *rosaria* and in the nominative singular, but a substantive is lacking. Presumably *cena* is understood (so the Loeb translator); *mitellita* would derive from *mitella*, a decorative headband which would be worn by all the guests, and *rosaria* would imply an equally lavish expenditure on roses.

28.1

ingenuorum paedagogia...nuptarum concubinatus: Suetonius now turns to examples of Nero's *libido*. His sexual vices are made the more disgraceful by the two contrasts; *paedagogia* were boy prostitutes of slave or freed status while Nero's boys were free born (*ingenui*); concubines were also normally of slave or freed status while Nero's were newly married free women. Nothing is known of Rubria.

Acten libertam...peierarent: Nero's affair with the freedwoman Claudia Acte was encouraged by Seneca and Burrus in order to emancipate him from his mother's domination; Nero seems to have been genuinely fond of her (Tacitus, *Ann.* 13.12.1). Dio, but not Tacitus, also has the story that Nero wanted to marry her, which was of course excluded because of her origin. She had been bought in Asia; the royal origin which was to be sworn to was apparently to be attributed to a supposed descent from the Attalids, kings of Pergamum until 133 BC, and Dio (61.7.1) alleges that she was actually adopted into the family. She survived Nero and clearly amassed considerable wealth: a substantial household of slaves and freedmen, and estates near Puteoli and in Sardinia are attested. She was among those who buried Nero after his suicide (see 50 below).

puerum Sporum...exosculans: this 'marriage' apparently took place during Nero's visit to Greece. It was alleged that the main reason was his likeness to Poppaea (Dio, 63.12.4-13) and the reference in Dio, 62.28.2ff. looks ahead to this event, *contra* Gallivan (1974) 309. Dio, in the latter reference, also contains a slightly different version of the joke quoted by Suetonius.

28.2

nam matris...affirmant: *nam* here is not explanatory but introduces a fresh point. The suggestion of incest between Nero and Agrippina occurs in our three main sources but uncharacteristically they all just manage to avoid committing themselves to saying that it actually happened (Tacitus, *Ann.* 14. 2; Dio, 61.11.4); note Suetonius' *nemo dubitavit* and *affirmant*. According to Tacitus, Fabius Rusticus said that the initiative was Nero's, and Suetonius follows this line; Cluvius Rufus and other authors said that Agrippina tried to seduce Nero but was prevented by Seneca through the influence of Acte. Suetonius combines this latter point with the notion of Nero's supposed responsibility. Dio has Agrippina as the instigator as well as the story of the concubine who looked like her.

29.1

suam quidem pudicitiam...a Doryphoro liberto: Dio, 63.13.2 is almost identical.

cui etiam...concessisse delicta: Suetonius has made an error here; the freedman in question was not Doryphorus but Pythagoras. There are similar accounts of the story in Dio, 62.28.3 and 63.13.2 and in Tacitus, *Ann.* 15.37.8-9, where it is dated to 64, shortly before the fire of Rome. For the death of Doryphorus, see 35 below.

30.1

divitiarum et pecuniae...modum tenuit: Suetonius now turns to Nero's *luxuria*, concentrating on his extravagance and conspicuous consumption. Imperial extravagance remained an easy target as long as the Roman Empire survived. The Elder Pliny has a number of examples from the principate of Nero scattered through the *N.H.*, some of which reappear in the historical sources. The prodigality of Gaius is described by Suetonius in *Caligula* 37; he is said to have got through in just two years the reserve of 2,700 million sesterces left by Tiberius.

Many might have agreed with Nero's view that wealth was there to be spent; the financial prudence of emperors like Galba and Vespasian brought little popularity and was easily portrayed as miserliness. It was hard for emperors to find a middle way in this matter.

30.2
in Tiridaten...contulit: for the visit of Tiridates and a discussion of Suetonius' separation of the good and bad aspects of it, see 13 above. *quod vix credibile videatur* seems to mean not the cost in itself but that the sum was spent on a client king.

Menecraten citharoedum: Menecrates was a teacher of the lyre and celebrated a 'triumph' for Nero after the latter's 'victory' in the *Neronia* of 65 (Dio, 63.1.1).

Spiculum murmillonem: John of Antioch (fg. 91) preserves from Dio a confused anecdote of a certain Spiculus described as prefect of the camp, i.e. praetorian prefect and killed by the praetorians when they deserted Nero. His office is certainly wrong but he may be the same man and one of Nero's bodyguards. Bradley (1978) seeks to identify the triumphators, presumably victims in the Pisonian or other conspiracies; the emphasis is on the contrast between such distinguished men and the recipients.

cercopithecum: the literal meaning is a 'long-tailed monkey'. It has been taken as a personal name, but it is probably a word of abuse for a freedman; see also Lucilius, 1337 (Krenkel); and see Introduction for Suetonius' (lost) monograph on the vocabulary of abuse.

30.3
canusinatis: Canusium (Canossa), was famous for its wool.

Mazacum: the Mazaces were a Numidian tribe famous for their cavalry; they would have given an exotic appearance to the cavalcade.

31.1

non in alia re tamen damnosior quam in aedificando: for Suetonius' normal attitude to building projects, see 16.1 above. Besides ignoring Nero's works of a traditional kind, he here concentrates on Nero's notorious new palace built after the fire of Rome, and on grandiose but unfinished projects. *damnosior*: here 'damaging' in an economic sense.

domum a Palatio...auream nominavit: the *domus transitoria* connected the imperial residence on the Palatine, which went back to Augustus and was probably not remarkable, with the gardens of Maecenas on the Esquiline, crossing the depression where the Colosseum now stands. It was destroyed in the fire and the Golden House (so named by Nero himself), was begun soon afterwards. Suetonius' description is the longest we have of it, Tacitus being impressionistic (*Ann.* 15.29.1 and 42.1). The architects and engineers of the scheme were named by Tacitus as Severus and Celer, *quibus ingenium et audacia erat quae natura negavisset per artem temptare.* It is clear that one of the biggest objections was the large area of parkland covered by the property right in the heart of Rome (125 acres is a modern estimate). Horace (*Odes* 3.1.33f.) had long ago objected to luxurious villas which involved the displacement of poor peasants. The creation of an artificial landscape with a lake, pavilions, cultivated land and a wild park is the realisation of the fantasy landscapes known from Pompeian wall paintings. The mechanical devices in the ceilings seem to be confirmed by Seneca (*Ep. Mor.* 90.15), who – without naming Nero – mentions others which were probably in the *domus transitoria*.

There is no reason to suppose that there was any religious or astrological significance in the fact that it rotated; Nero loved ingenious gadgets, *incredibilium cupitor* as Tacitus called him. The palace also contained art treasures seized in the Greek world (Pliny, *N.H.* 34.84). It may never have been finished; Vespasian built the Colosseum on the site of the lake and the Baths of Titus occupied some of the park. Much of the building was destroyed by fire in 104. Some parts were incorporated in the substructure of Trajan's Baths and their decoration caused a sensation when they were discovered during the Renaissance. See Boethius (1961) and Dudley (1967) 138ff.

in quo colossus: Pliny (*N.H.* 34.45) says it was of bronze and made by the sculptor Zenodorus. It was altered by Vespasian to represent the Sun. It was the first of several colossal statues of emperors, including Trajan, to be erected at Rome. Substantial fragments of that of Constantine (in marble) survive.

31.2

albulis: from Aquae Albulae, sulphur springs near Tibur.

31.3

incohabat piscinam...converteretur: nothing else is known of such an enormous project; such a pool would have been several miles long.

fossam ab Averno...praeceperat: the coast between the Bay of Naples and Ostia was dangerous. Corn ships put in at Puteoli and their cargoes were transhipped up the coast; 200 were wrecked off Ostia in 62. A century earlier Julius Caesar had planned a canal to run from the lower Tiber to Terracina in a similar scheme to lessen the coastal voyage. Nero's plan, designed by the architects of the Golden House (Tacitus, *Ann.* 14.42.2-4), was even more impressive. The actual length has been exaggerated by Suetonius; it would have been about 135 English (125 Roman) miles. It was abandoned at Nero's death, though parts had been excavated; see Pliny, *N.H.* 14.61.

etiam scelere convictos: execution would have been the penalty in most cases.

31.4

spe quadam...molientium opera: Nero's informant was Caesellius Bassus, who came from North Africa; the incident was in 65; see also Tacitus, *Ann.* 16.1ff.

32.1

verum ut spes fefellit...intendit animum: Suetonius here turns to Nero's *avaritia*, an excessive desire for money (see also *Galba* 12.1). If it is true that the pay of the army and the allocation of bounties to veterans fell into arrears, this might explain the disloyalty of some army units in the final crisis of the reign, but the point is not otherwise attested. Though Nero's financial difficulties cannot have been caused simply by his disappointed expectations of Dido's treasure, chronologically Suetonius is roughly correct in dating them to the later part of his principate. Ironically, in 62 Nero had criticised earlier emperors for undertaking excessive expenditure in advance of income and had set up a commission of senior senators to look into the imperial revenue, presumably to increase the efficiency of collection, since no general increase of tribute is alleged (Tacitus, *Ann.* 15.19.4). The commission may also (but this is not stated) have had something to do with a major change in the monetary system in 64, known from numismatics but ignored by all our literary sources. The imperial gold coins (*aurei*) were now minted at the rate of 45 instead of 42 to the pound of gold, and *denarii* at 96 instead of 84 to the pound of silver. The reduction in weight naturally brought a profit to the treasury.

In 38 Suetonius associates Nero's financial exactions with the cost of rebuilding in Rome after the fire, and Tacitus (*Ann.* 15.45.1ff.) and Dio (62.18.5) concur. There is no need to assume a general economic crisis; in spite of appearances the Roman empire lived fiscally from hand to mouth and sudden demands for extraordinary expenditures always created problems. Delays in paying the army and in making provision for soldiers due for discharge (two separate items) could only be temporary expedients without serious consequences. Retaining men past their normal terms of service had caused a mutiny at the start of Tiberius' reign. The only means of cutting imperial expenditure was in the manner in which the emperor lived. Since Nero apparently did not change his ways, an alternative method of covering expenditure was to resort to confiscatory measures affecting the wealthy. The list of categories in 32.2 is suspect as being highly generalised. Bradley (1978) has an extensive note concluding that there is little evidence for the charges.

32.2

ante omnia...quas ipse contingeret: Nero claimed five-sixths instead of half the estates of freedmen who bore the names of families with which he himself was connected, unless they could show that they had a genuine right; presumably Claudii, Domitii, Antonii and perhaps Julii would all be included. Nothing is known from other sources about this. Strictly speaking it was a private matter within the imperial household.

ingratorum...dictasset ea: beginning with Augustus, legacies were of profound importance to the emperor's finances; it was an extension of the Republican practice whereby politicians made bequests to political friends and allies. Under Augustus it was regarded as axiomatic that men who had enjoyed his favour should remember him in their wills (Valerius Maximus, 18.8.6). Not only senators but prominent men of lower social ranks were already under strong pressure to do the same under Gaius; see Millar (1977) 153ff.

lege maiestate...tenerentur: during the first century, confiscation of property became part of the penalty for serious crimes and above all for treason. Since most of those convicted for treason were of senatorial or equestrian rank, the *fiscus* thus obtained substantial windfalls. Allegations of more or less indiscriminate attacks on the rich, though not by means of trumped up treason trials, are alleged by Suetonius against Tiberius and Gaius (*Tiberius* 49; *Caligula* 41). As regards Nero, his allegation is tendentious for the period before the Pisonian consipiracy of 65 and is at first sight at variance with his statement (39.1 below) that Nero was surprisingly tolerant of verbal criticism. The narrative of Tacitus however does support the view that after the Pisonian conspiracy a number of trumped up charges of treason were made, and Dio (63.11.1-3) associates the worst examples with the period of Nero's tour of Greece.

32.3

revocavit praemia...detulissent: although an unusual expression this seems to imply that Nero had rewarded those cities which had awarded him prizes in the various competitions, and now cancelled whatever he had granted them. Nothing else is known of such rewards; the freedom given to Achaia is certainly not meant, since it was revoked by Vespasian, not Nero.

32.4

ultimo templis...Galba restituit: the reference to the *di Penates* shows that Suetonius has in mind the temples in Rome, though nothing is known of the specific case. Tacitus (*Ann.* 15.45.2) is highly rhetorical: *spoliatis in urbe templis egestoque auro quod triumphis, quod votis omnis populi Romani aetas prospere aut in metu sacraverat*; see also Dio, 63.11.3. The better-attested looting of temples in the Greek world also comes after the fire at Rome (Tacitus, *Ann.* 15.45.2; Pausanias, 10.7.1, 6.25.9 and 26.3; Pliny, *N.H.* 34.84).

33.1

parricidia et caedes a Claudio exorsus est...neglexit: by far the longest list of Nero's crimes involve his *saevitia*, no doubt the worst element in his principate in the eyes of Suetonius, although murders within the imperial family tended to be viewed in a different light from executions or forced suicides of members of the Senate.

Claudius died on 13 October 54. In *Claudius* 44 Suetonius notes several versions of his death which differ in detail, but the main story of the poisoning, for which Agrippina was held responsible, was almost universally believed (Tacitus, *Ann.* 12.66f.; Dio, 60.34; Pliny, *N.H.* 22.92; Martial, 1.21.4; Juvenal, 5.147 and 6.620). Only Josephus (*A.J.* 20.8.1) calls it a report. Nero's joke, found also in Dio, is not evidence – though contemporaries clearly thought it was. Tacitus says that Claudius was taken ill before poison was administered.

morari: a play on the Greek word μωρός, 'stupid'. It is not clear which *decreta et constituta* are meant other than those criticised in the 'programme speech'.

33.2

Britannicum...adgressus est: Suetonius does not repeat the story he gives in *Claudius* 43, that Claudius had been preparing to re-establish Britannicus when he died (Dio, 60.34.1). This is quite possible; Britannicus would have been 14 (the age at which Nero had been granted adult status) on 12 February 55, and it is perhaps significant that Britannicus died shortly before this date (Tacitus, *Ann.* 13.15.1ff.). The words *ne quandoque...praevaleret* hint at the true reason for his removal, assuming that the official story of his death through an epileptic fit is false. Claudius had been officially deified and, in spite of the mockery which the event no doubt aroused at court, exemplified in Seneca's *Apocolocyntosis*, it could have worked in Britannicus' interest; there may have been some to whom the claims to the succession for the first time of a son born to the previous emperor seemed reasonable. According to Josephus (*A.J.* 20.153), who doubted whether Claudius had been poisoned, few at the time knew that the death of Britannicus was also unnatural and some eight years later the people of Amisos in Pontus apparently did not even know he was dead (*AE* (1959) 224). There are obvious similarities to the removal of possible rivals to Tiberius (Agrippa Postumus) and to Gaius (Tiberius Gemellus).

quod acceptum...discipulos dedit: Tacitus (*Ann.* 13.15 and 16) has a basically similar account, though he is more interested in the events at the dinner party than in Lucusta; see also Dio, 61.7.4. Lucusta is apparently the correct form of the name, though the MSS of Tacitus have Locusta. According to Tacitus she had been involved in the death of Claudius and Dio (64.3.4) says she was put to death by Galba.

legem Juliam: this looks careless – no *Lex Julia* applicable to the circumstances is known.

34.1

matrem facta...gravabatur: the murder of Agrippina remained, along with the fire, the most notorious incident of Nero's principate, our three main sources all giving a basically similar story at some length. The reasons for Nero's crime are variously handled, however. The main tradition (Tacitus and Dio) attributes it to Agrippina's opposition to Nero's infatuation with Poppaea Sabina but there are objections to this (see 35.3 below); in places other than the actual description of the murder, Tacitus (*Ann.* 12.62.2 and 13.13.3), like Suetonius, asserts the domineering attitude of Agrippina towards her son during 54 and 55. There is no reason to doubt that the tradition of Agrippina's desire to enjoy real power through her son is correct.

Rhodumque abiturus: there is no other evidence for this story; the mention of Rhodes might indicate that Nero made some sarcastic remark which referred to the withdrawal of Tiberius to Rhodes in 6 BC.

mox et honori...expulit: this was in 55; Tacitus, *Ann.* 13.18.4-5 is very similar; see also Dio, 61.8.4. Agrippina lost to Burrus and Seneca in the struggle for influence over Nero's public activity fairly early, but it seems that she continued to have the means of interfering in his private life. She took up residence in the house which had formerly belonged to her grandmother, the younger Antonia.

Germanorum: Augustus had formed a bodyguard of German horsemen, and the tradition evidently continued.

neque in divexando...inquietarent: nothing is known of these stories, but the first may have some reference to the incident described in Tacitus, *Ann.* 13.19-22. In 55, taking advantage of the apparent decline in Agrippina's fortunes, Junia Silana, a connection of the imperial family and once a close friend of Agrippina, accused her of trying to instigate Rubellius Plautus, a descendent of Tiberius, to rebel and of intending to marry him. The accusation was supported by Nero's aunt Domitia. Tacitus says that Nero was with difficulty restrained from condemning his mother, but makes no suggestion that he had anything to do with the charge itself. In fact Agrippina not only vindicated herself but obtained the exile of Silana and her helpers.

34.2
verum minis...statuit: nothing specific is said in our sources to illustrate Agrippina's threatening attitude from 55-59. Probably she attempted to restrain Nero's enthusiasm for singing and chariot racing; Tacitus (*Ann.* 14.13.3), in spite of what he says about the influence of Poppaea on Nero's decision to undertake the crime, gives as its main result his plunging headlong into these activities: *quas male coercitas qualiscumque matris reverentia tardaverat.*

et cum ter...antidotis praemunitam: Suetonius cheerfully asserts what Tacitus more prudently thinks was Nero's original idea, rejected on various grounds, but he too says she had taken antidotes.

lacunaria...paravit: not otherwise known, but perhaps to be taken with the collapsible ship (see below) and the revolving ceilings of the Golden House as appropriate to Nero as the addict of mechanical contrivances.

solutilem navem...morte vitasset: see the very similar narratives, though with a few variant details, in Tacitus, *Ann.* 14.1-8 and Dio, 61.12-13. The *Quinquatrus* (also *Quinguatria*) were four festival days (19-23 March) in honour of Minerva. Agrippina had been staying at Antium. Dio differs from Suetonius in saying that

Nero accompanied her from Antium in the fatal ship in order to allay any suspicion. The villa in which Nero was staying and to which he invited her (*evocavit*) to dinner was at Baiae, while Agrippina was to stay the night at another imperial property at Bauli. She went to the dinner in a litter (so Tacitus) but began the return journey in the ship. Characteristically Suetonius narrates the whole story from Nero's standpoint, while Tacitus gives as much to Agrippina. Suetonius also ignores the summoning of Seneca and Burrus (who were perhaps ignorant of the plot), their ineffectiveness when it seemed to be going wrong, and the entrusting of the actual killing to the freedman Anicetus (35.2 below), prefect of the fleet at Misenum.

trierarchis: a trierarch commanded a trireme or a *liburnica*; one named Herculius accompanied Anicetus to kill Agrippina after she reached the shore.

34.4

adduntur his...oborta bibisse: according to Dio (61.14.3), he looked over her body and said 'I did not know I had such a beautiful mother'. Tacitus (*Ann.* 14.9.1) leaves the question open as does Suetonius.

quamquam et militum...confirmaretur: the official story was in effect summed up in the previous subsection in the words *quasi deprehensum crimen voluntaria morte vitasset*; Tacitus describes Burrus organizing the praetorian officers to congratulate Nero on his 'escape' while Seneca wrote to the Senate an account of Agrippina's guilt, accompanied by an attack on her whole record including her actions under Claudius. Tacitus may be right in suggesting that the story was not believed, though this is not to say that there was sympathy with Agrippina, whose strong personality had made her many enemies; compare the remark attributed to Domitian: *condicionem principum miserrimum, quibus de coniuratione comperta non crederetur nisi occisis* (*Domitian* 21).

quin et facto...exorare temptavit: according to the Elder Pliny (*N.H.* 30.14), who was extremely hostile to the 'religion of the Magi' (meaning in general magical practices which he believed all derived from Parthia), Nero was initiated into its secrets by Tiridates who was accompanied on his visit to Rome by some Magi; he was enthusiastic about it until it failed to provide him with the magical and occult powers he had hoped for.

peregrinatione quidem...non ausus est: Dio (63.14.4) has a similar allegation saying that he omitted a visit to Athens 'because of the story of the Furies'. Suetonius' reference to Nero's fear of the Furies is presumably connected; the point was that the Furies were particularly concerned to avenge murders in a family. The concept of the Furies (Greek *Erinyes*) was originally purely Greek and the anecdote, if true, is another manifestation of Nero's deep involvement in Greek culture.

34.5

iunxit parricidio...ne quid abscederet: this refers to Domitia, not (Domitia) Lepida, for whom see 7 above. A story of rivalry between her and Agrippina is in Tacitus (*Ann.* 13.19.4), which presumably derived from the fact that Passienus Crispus had divorced her in order to marry Agrippina. Dio (61.17.1) has the same allegation as Suetonius, but Tacitus does not refer to her death, no doubt believing the anecdote to be baseless; it occurred in 59 as the reference to Nero's first beard indicates.

35.1

Statiliam Messalinam...trucidavit: according to the Scholiast on Juvenal 6.434, Statilia Messalina *opibus et forma et ingenio plurimam valuit*; all these factors must have counted because she had already been married four times before she married Nero. Her great-grandfather was the distinguished general of Augustus, T. Statilius Taurus, consul in 37 and 26 BC and triumphator in 34 BC. Her fourth husband M. Julius Vestinus Atticus was consul in 65, the year of the Pisonian conspiracy. Tacitus (Ann. 15.52.5) says that he was not brought into the conspiracy because Piso feared his *acre ingenium*; nevertheless Nero ordered him to commit suicide while dealing with the conspiracy, on the grounds of *vetus odium*. The real motive can hardly be determined. The marriage took place some time in 66. She survived Nero, and Otho is said to have wanted to marry her.

Octaviae consuetudinem...a se fateretur: the brief version of the death of Octavia given by Suetonius is on the same lines as the extended treatment in Tacitus (*Ann.* 14.60-64) and avoids some of the difficulties of the latter's narrative. The divorce took place in the first half of 62 in regular form but Octavia was shortly afterwards sent to Campania under house arrest. Popular feeling in her favour was certainly displayed and there is no doubt that the opposition to the divorce, which had been led by Burrus till his death, was based on good grounds; marriage to the daughter of Claudius was politically important. But the popular discontent led to her removal from Italy and banishment to the island of Pandateria, already notorious in the fate of other imperial ladies; Julia, daughter of Augustus, had died there in 14, Agrippina the elder in 33, and Julia, daughter of Germanicus, in 41. Tacitus says that most, though not all, Octavia's slaves remained faithful under torture; see also Dio, 62.13 and Josephus, *A.J.* 20.153. Her character, as one of the few sympathetic members of the dynasty, and her innocence, made her an appropriate heroine for the tragedy *Octavia*, traditionally attributed to Seneca.

35.3

Poppaeam duodecimo die...incesserat: the father of Poppaea was a certain T. Ollius who never got beyond equestrian rank because he had been a friend of Sejanus. She took the name of her maternal grandfather T. Poppaeus Sabinus, consul in 9. Her first husband, the *eques Romanus* (35.1), was Rufrius Crispinus, praetorian prefect from 47 until he was dismissed in 51 on the instigation of Agrippina. Suetonius ignores the origins of Poppaea's affair with Nero, which are obscure. In *Otho* 3.1 he follows the story, found also in Tacitus, *Hist.* 1.13.3, Dio, 61.11.2 and Plutarch, *Galba* 19f., to the effect that Nero fell in love with Poppaea at an unspecified date, forced Rufrius Crispinus to divorce her and entrusted her to his friend Otho to facilitate the affair. At this point there are divergences: whether or not she was married to Otho (Suetonius says *nuptiarum specie*); whether Otho was given a governorship in Spain because he was in love with Poppaea himself and resented Nero; or whether the latter merely suspected Otho as a rival for Poppaea. Tacitus (*Ann.* 13.45ff.) takes a different and much simpler line, that Otho himself seduced Poppaea when she was the wife of Crispinus and married her after a divorce; only then did Nero get to know her and send Otho to Spain in 58 to get him out of the way. This version, being written later than that in the *Histories*, is normally regarded as a correction by Tacitus of his earlier version and based on better information. This may be so, but Tacitus seems to be wrong in portraying Poppaea as urging Nero on to murder Agrippina as an obstacle to their marriage, since he did not divorce Octavia until three years after the death of his mother. The marriage to Poppaea was in May 62. She was pregnant at the time and her daughter was born about 21 January 63. She died in 65. Tacitus, *Ann.* 16.6 and Dio, 62.27.4 give the same cause (but without her nagging). According to Dio (63.26.4), one of Nero's last acts in the final weeks of his reign in 68 was the consecration of a temple dedicated to the goddess Sabina Aphrodite; see also *ILS* 233. Coinage of Corinth also celebrates her deification, with that of her daughter (Smallwood (1967) no.148).

ex hac filiam...infantem: Claudia Augusta died when only 4 months old and was deified (Tacitus, *Ann.* 15.23.4).

35.4

nullum adeo...perculerit: Suetonius now widens the list of Nero's victims from his immediate to more distant relatives and connections.

Antoniam Claudi filiam...interemit: Claudia Antonia was Claudius' daughter by his second wife Aelia Paetina, and named after Claudius' mother the younger Antonia. In 41 (after Claudius' accession) she was married to Cn. Pompeius

Magnus, a descendant of Caesar's rival. Pompeius was executed by Claudius some time before 47, after which she was married to Faustus Cornelius Sulla Felix, a descendant of the dictator; see Syme (1939) Stemma V. In 55 an allegation that Burrus was plotting to remove Nero in favour of Sulla was rejected out of hand (Tacitus, *Ann.* 13.23). However, in spite of his dull and unenterprising character, Sulla was exiled in 58 and killed in 62 (Tacitus, *Ann.* 13.47.1 and 14.57.4). It was said by Pliny that Antonia was to be used as a pawn in the Pisonian conspiracy, a detail about which Tacitus (*Ann.* 15.53.4-5) had serious doubts. It is not impossible that Nero did consider trying to strengthen his dynastic position by a marriage to Claudius' surviving daughter. Her death is not mentioned in the surviving portion of Tacitus so presumably it took place in 66 or later.

ceteros...coniunctos: Suetonius has not named a number of relations of Nero who were killed because they were or seemed to be a threat to his position. Three of them were, like Nero himself, direct descendants of Augustus: M. Junius Silanus killed in 54 (Tacitus, *Ann.* 13.1), though in this case Agrippina was responsible; his brother D. Junius Silanus Torquatus in 64 (*Ann.* 15.35.2-3); and his son L. Junius Silanus Torquatus in 65 (*Ann.* 16.9.2-5). Rubellius Plautus, killed in 62, was a descendant of Tiberius (*Ann.* 14.57). Their deaths testify to the importance of the hereditary factor in Rome at the time.

Aulum Plautium iuvenem: this is hard to explain. *PW* XXI (I) 29 suggests that he was the son of Aulus Plautius, the conqueror of Britain who had received from Claudius an *ovatio*, a rare honour for a private citizen. The charge made in 57 that the latter's wife Pomponia Graeca was addicted to an *externa superstitio* may have a connection (Tacitus, *Ann.* 13.32) but it is not clear how he was related to Nero by blood or marriage, unless the fact that a relative of the elder Plautius, Plautia Urgulanilla, had been Claudius' first wife is meant. Tacitus has no reference to the matter, which must have taken place before 59.

35.5

Rufrium Crispinum Poppaea natum: this too is otherwise unknown.

Tuscum nutricis filium: C. Caecina Tuscus is known as a *iuridicus Alexandreae et Aegypti* in 51-52 under Claudius. According to Fabius Rusticus, Seneca dissuaded Nero from making him praetorian prefect in 55 (Tacitus, *Ann.* 13.20). He was prefect of Egypt late in Nero's principate but before 66, and survived his exile; see Dio, 62.18.

Senecam praeceptorem: for the position of Seneca, see 7 above. He was ordered to commit suicide in 65 after the suppression of the Pisonian conspiracy, in which he was not implicated, though his nephew the poet Lucan had been (Tacitus, *Ann.* 15.60ff.). In a dramatised version of an interview between Nero and Seneca in 62, at which the latter sought to retire, Tacitus (*Ann.* 14.53-56) also makes much of Seneca's offer to surrender to Nero his vast wealth, and Nero's assurances of goodwill. See also Dio (62.24 and 25), who believed that Seneca was a leader of the conspiracy.

Burro praefecto: this is Suetonius' only mention of Sextus Afranius Burrus. A native of Vasio (Vaison) in Gallia Narbonensis, he had been a military tribune and a procurator of Livia, Tiberius and Claudius before he was made praetorian prefect under Claudius in 51, through the influence of Agrippina. He held the post until his death in 62. Tacitus (*Ann.* 13.2) emphasises the remarkable harmony which existed between him and Seneca from 54 to 62 and that the two men were the main directors of policy through this period should not be seriously questioned. In the case of Burrus it was no doubt his integrity and experience in finance and administration rather than his military experience which made him effective. Suetonius has omitted an account of his influence for the same reason as in the case of Seneca, that it does not fall within his concept of biographical relevance. Like Dio (62.13.3), he believed the story that Nero poisoned him; Tacitus (*Ann.* 14.51.1-3) says that this is uncertain but clearly inclines to what was the majority view of his sources.

libertos divites...indito intercepit: Suetonius seems to be generalising from a single instance again, and states as a fact what was doubted by Tacitus (*Ann.* 14.65.1) in a very similar passage (dated to 62): *libertorum potissimos veneno interfecisse creditus est, Doryphorum quasi adversatum nuptiis Poppaeae, Pallantem, quod immensam pecuniam longa senecta detineret.*

M. Antonius Pallas was a slave of the younger Antonia, then freed by her; he was *a rationibus* under Claudius and notoriously the most powerful and the richest of his freedmen (*Claudius* 28). A figure of 400 million sesterces is given by Dio (62.14. 3) for his fortune. He had supported the marriage of Agrippina to Claudius and the adoption of Nero. He was removed from his position by Nero in 55 but there is no good evidence that Nero was really hostile to him; see Tacitus, *Ann.* 13.14.1. and 13.23; Josephus, *A.J.* 20.182. According to Dio (61.5.4), Doryphorus is said to have received 10 million sesterces from Nero while apparently in the post of *a libellis*. On the death of a freedman, the *patronus* would be able to claim a share in his estate equivalent to that of one child if the freedman was survived by less than three children.

36.1

foris et in exteros: outside his family and household, in contrast to the victims mentioned earlier. Note that those mentioned in 35.4 and 5, the son of his nurse, his *praeceptor*, his praetorian prefect and his freedmen are all regarded as in some sense particularly close to Nero, though strictly only the *liberti* were part of his household.

stella crinita: during Nero's principate an unusually large number of comets were observed; Pliny (*N.H.* 2.92) says they were almost continuous. Correlation with Chinese annals indicates that there were six; see Rogers (1953) 240ff. The one mentioned by Suetonius appears by its association with the Pisonian conspiracy to be that of mid-64.

ex Balbillo astrologi: possibly the famous astrologer in whose honour Vespasian allowed Ephesus to hold a festival (Dio, 66.9.2) but unlikely to be the Claudius Balbillus known as prefect of Egypt in 55.

prior maiorque Pisoniana Romae: by far the best known of the conspiracies directed against members of the Julio-Claudian dynasty, thanks to an account in great detail in Tacitus, 15.48-74. Its object was to kill Nero and replace him by C. Calpurnius Piso, a member of an old Republican family but not the originator of the plot. Various motives, good and bad, are given by Tacitus for the participation of various individuals, but a general anger at the degradation of the imperial position by Nero's theatrical activities seems to have been the most prominent. The plot was revealed through incompetence in April 65. In the punishment of those involved, nineteen deaths and thirteen exiles are recorded by name in Tacitus. It is not clear why Suetonius should ignore them all while he mentions other deaths (37.1 below). From Nero's point of view the most serious aspect of the plot was not the participation of disgruntled senators but that of some officers of the praetorian guard. See also Dio, 62.24 and 27.

posterior Viniciana Benevento conflata: Suetonius' reference is the only one to this plot, which presumably occurred in 67, where Tacitus' account has not survived. It probably derived its name from Annius Vinicianus, son-in-law of Corbulo. Vinicianus had led the escort of Tiridates on his visit to Rome in 66. His family had a record of opposition; his brother Annius Pollio had been exiled for complicity in the Pisonian conspiracy and his father had not only been a leader in the plot which removed Gaius but also had a hand in the rebellion of Scribonianus against Claudius in 42. The object of the plot of 67 may have been to make Corbulo emperor; at any rate when Nero was in Greece, Corbulo was summoned there from the East and ordered to commit suicide as soon as he arrived; see Dio, 63.17.6.

coniurati...prohibitos quaerere: the details about the defendant being loaded with chains, and the fate of the children of those condemned are not known elsewhere, but probably refer to the Pisonian conspiracy in view of the following point.

nonnulli etiam imputarent: i.e. they made a boast of their participation. Tacitus gives two examples, both of praetorian officers who did this. One was named Sulpicius Asper who, when asked why he joined the plot, replied *non aliter tot flagitiis eius subveniri potuisse* (*Ann.* 15.68); Dio (62.24.2) makes the remark even more epigrammatic; ἄλλως σοι βοηθῆσαι οὐκ ἐδυνάμην– 'I could help you in no other way'. Presumably Suetonius feared his readers might miss the irony and so explained the point.

37.1

nullus posthac...quacumque de causa: the chronological point is of some importance, though *posthac* really refers to the Pisonian conspiracy rather than that of Vinicianus. In spite of general accusations, Nero did not act with the ruthlessness of suspicion and fear till after the former had revealed widespread disaffection in both senate and equestrian ranks. Nearly all earlier executions of senators can be explained by their membership of, or connection with, the imperial family. After the conspiracy Nero began to strike out at various men thought to be dangerous either because their high social standing or their positions as army commanders made them a potential threat, or because they had personal qualities which made them unafraid to show disapproval of him.

sed ne de pluribus referam: Suetonius omits to name three army commanders obliged to commit suicide in Greece where they had been summoned by Nero, Corbulo and two brothers, Sulpicius Scribonius Rufus and Sulpicius Scribonius Proculus, governors of Upper and Lower Germany; see Warmington (1969) 140-141 and 155ff.

Salvidieno Orfito: his full name was Sergius Cornelius Salvidienus Orfitus, consul in 51. The trivial grounds alleged are given in almost identical words (but without Salvidienus being named) in Dio, 62.27.1. No doubt their common source derived the point from the prosecution of Salvidienus which would have argued suspicious behaviour in the political heart of Rome.

69

civitatibus ad stationem: as lodgings for delegates to Rome from Italian or provincial cities. Such patronage by a senator, particularly since the property was near the forum, was by this date unacceptable to the emperor.

Cassio Longino: the distinguished jurist C. Cassius Longinus, now old and blind, was first forbidden to attend the funeral of Poppaea by Nero, who then wrote to the senate demanding his exile along with that of his nephew and adopted son L. Junius Silanus; see Tacitus, *Ann.* 16.7-9. Cassius was married to Silanus' aunt Junia Lepida. Tacitus first argues that the reason for the attack on Cassius was his ancestral wealth and high moral character, but then says that in his letter to the senate Nero charged *quod inter imagines maiorum etiam C. Cassi effigiem coluisset, ita inscriptum 'duci partium'*. Dio (62.27.2) also mentions the possession of the image of the tyrannicide (Cassius) as the cause of the death of an unnamed person, obviously Longinus. In 65 Silanus was killed in Italy but Cassius was exiled to Sardinia; contrary to the implication of all three sources, he appears to have survived his exile and died in the time of Vespasian; see Pomponius, *Digest* 1.2.2.52. It was natural that Brutus and Cassius should be honoured by men of republican sentiments (Pliny, *Epistles* 1.17; Juvenal 5.36) but in Cassius' case he would be following normal aristocratic practice in honouring an ancestor. Equally naturally the practice could be regarded as provocative by emperors; under Tiberius a historian had been convicted for calling the two tyrannicides the last of the Romans (*Tiberius* 61.3).

Paeto Thraseae: P. Clodius Thrasea Paetus was the best known of the small but influential group whose opposition to Nero was to a considerable degree based on moral grounds derived from Stoic philosophy. The charges made against him and the circumstances of his death are described in detail by Tacitus, *Ann.* 16.21-35; see also Dio, 62.26. He seems to have been in high standing during the period when Seneca was influential, holding the consulship in 56; but in 59 he had walked out of the senate rather than participate in passing thanksgiving decrees for Nero's 'escape' from Agrippina's plot. In 62, however, he led the senate successfully in opposing the death penalty for a senator accused of writing abusive verses against Nero. In 63 Nero formally broke off friendly relations with him and he withdrew from public life. This and other matters including his lack of enthusiasm for Nero's musical performances were brought up in 66 at the time of Tiridates' visit and made the basis of a criminal charge. Above all, the leader of the prosecution, Cossutianus Capito, portrayed Thrasea as dividing the state and opposing Nero in the same way as Cato had opposed Julius Caesar. In the speech Tacitus puts into Capito's mouth occurs the passage *et habet sectatores vel potius satellites qui nondum contumaciam sententiarum sed habitum* *vultumque eius sectantur, rigidi et tristes*; this looks like a rhetorical version of a common source which Suetonius represents by *tristior et paedagogi vultus*. The detail, however trivial in appearance, pinpointed the fact of Thrasea's Stoicism, since followers of the sect affected, or were said to affect, an over-solemn demeanour, see Quintilian, 1.15 (*philosophi vultum et tristitiam et dissentientem a ceteris habitum*) and Martial 11.2.1. Thrasea committed suicide in a manner which displayed his courage and constancy and which was appropriate as an example to others. On the whole question of Stoicism under Nero, see Griffin (1976) and Warmington (1969) 142-154.

37.2

mori iussis: although there is no doubt that many of Nero's victims were innocent of conspiring against him, his *saevitia* had limits; members of the senate at least were generally permitted to commit suicide rather than suffer the indignity of execution. This privilege was not however granted to persons of lower social rank.

creditur etiam...obicere: nothing else is known of this extraordinary tale, to which even Suetonius does not fully commit himself.

37.3

ne reliquis quidem...libertis permissurum: it is characteristic of Suetonius' social deference that he regards as an enormity the possibility of transferring the provincial governorships from the senators to the *equites* (of which he was one) and freedmen. The story may have had its basis in an angry remark of Nero's late in his reign when he was certainly reciprocating the senate's hostility to him; Dio (63.15.1) has a story of a courtier who joked with him 'I hate you, Caesar, because you are a senator'. But there is no evidence of equestrians replacing senators, and freedmen, apart perhaps from Helius, were less influential than they had been under Claudius. In fact it can be regarded as showing how deeply entrenched socially and economically the senate was that no emperor, however bad his relations with it were, ever felt able to proceed on the lines alleged by Suetonius in the case of Nero.

dissimulata senatus mentione: no evidence exists for the form of the proclamation, but according to Dio (63.14.4), when Nero's victories were announced at the various competitions during his tour of Greece, the words were 'Nero Caesar wins this contest and crowns the Roman people and his own universe.' If the form of words was something like this, an objection to leaving out a mention of the senate was pure prejudice.

38.1

sed nec populo...incendit urbem: the great fire of Rome which broke out on 19 July 64 was the worst of many in Rome's history (there had been two as recently as the principate of Tiberius). It was an important feature of the tradition hostile to Nero. Tacitus (*Ann.* 15.38ff.) has a full account, as has Dio (62.16ff.), the latter highly rhetorical. As is well known, only Tacitus even suggests the possibility that Nero was not responsible by the words *forte an dolo principis incertum*, though the more discreditable version is what is left in the mind of the reader. Nero's responsibility was accepted by the Elder Pliny, *N.H.* 27.5. Tacitus appears to combine two versions, one of which stressed Nero's activity in organising relief work. Suetonius betrays one reason why it was plausible to blame Nero; his regulations for a better planned city which were subsequently introduced (see 16 above) easily led to the proposition that he had set fire to the city because he disliked its old fashioned inconvenience. Suetonius cheerfully asserts this (*quasi* here does not mean 'as if' but is causal) in spite of the fact that he listed the building regulations among the good aspects of Nero's principate. Tacitus (*Ann.* 15.40.3) cunningly inserts the idea into the middle of his account: *plusque infamiae id incendium habuit quia praediis Tigellini Aemilianis proruperat videbaturque Nero condendae urbis novae et cognomento suo appellandae gloriam quaerere.* At the start of the passage Suetonius emphasised the solemnity of the occasion by the use of the word *patria* for Rome. It is interesting that when Tacitus comes to describe the aftermath of the fire and the building of the Golden House he says *usus est patriae ruinis;* perhaps both have a verbal reminiscence of their common source. The author and title of the Greek tragedy from which the line is taken are unknown. 'When I am dead let the earth be consumed by fire', which Nero caps by saying, 'No, when I am alive'. The line was well known: Cic. *de Fin.* 3.19.64 and Seneca *de Clem.* 2.2.2.

plerique consulares...non attigerent: the allegation that persons were observed spreading the fire is put in a less definite form by Tacitus; the obvious explanation is common looting, if not an official attempt to create fire-breaks.

circa domum Auream: anachronistic, but presumably referring to a piece of property subsequently included in the palace grounds.

38.2

per sex dies: so Tacitus, *Ann.* 15.40.1, but a further outbreak of three days followed (15.40.3).

praeter immensum numerum...duraverat: the destruction of the ancient monuments of Rome is described in a very similar passage in Tacitus who names some of the temples dating from the time of the kings of Rome. There is no reason to doubt this, but the Forum, Capitol and part of the Palatine escaped, and the chief losses were no doubt in the residential areas, both among the appartment blocks where the poor lived (*immensum numerum insularum*) and in areas where individual houses of the wealthy (*domus*) preponderated; for the perils of overcrowded *insulae,* see Martial 1.117 and Juvenal 3 *passim.*

e turra Maecenatiana...decantavit: the unforgettable image of Nero 'fiddling while Rome burned' is found in our three sources, but with variations. The title of Nero's poem is the same in all, but Dio (62.18.1) locates Nero on the roof of his palace, while Tacitus (*Ann.* 15.39.3) puts the performance in his private theatre.

Halosin Ilii: the Capture of Troy – transliterated Greek; it may have been in that language. Juvenal (8.221) regarded the work as one more objection to Nero.

38.3
ac ne non hinc...permisit: that property owners were kept away from their damaged homes for a while is quite possible and would have been reasonable. Suetonius maliciously implies that Nero's agents would loot the properties while their owners were absent. Tacitus (*Ann.* 15.43.2) confirms that he promised to pay for the removal of debris.

conlationibus non receptis...exhausit: Dio, 62.18.4-5 is very similar and Tacitus (*Ann.* 15.45.1ff.) also refers to exactions throughout the empire following the fire. No doubt some communities anticipated inevitable pressures. One figure is known; Lugdunum (Lyons) contributed 4 million sesterces which Nero returned some two years later when Lugdunum itself suffered from some disaster, presumably a fire; see Tacitus, *Ann.* 16.13.5.

39.1
accesserunt...fortuita: it is interesting to note that Suetonius does not hold Nero responsible even indirectly for the disasters in Britain and Armenia.

pestilentia: this occurred in 65. It may be noted that Suetonius, like Tacitus (*Ann.* 16.13.1-3), introduces his description of the plague as a sort of supplement to the crimes which occurred in 65: *tot facinoribus foedum annum etiam dii tempestatibus et morbis insignivere.* The arrangement may well go back to their common source.

Libitina: the goddess of corpses. In her temple, requisites for funerals could be bought or hired, and a register of deaths was kept.

in rationem venerunt: 'were entered in the register'.

clades Britannica...direpta sunt: the reference is to the revolt of Boudicca; see note on 18 above. The full accounts are in Tacitus, *Ann.* 14.29-39 and Dio, 62.1-12. Dio refers to two 'Roman cities' destroyed and Tacitus names the *colonia* Camulodunum (Colchester); Verulamium (near St. Albans), described as a *municipium*; and Londinium (London), very important but not a *colonia*. It may be that Dio and Suetonius are considering only the towns of Roman or, in the case of Verulamium, more likely Latin status. Tacitus gives the number massacred as 70,000, Dio as 80,000, both mentioning Roman citizens and allies.

ignominia...Syria retenta: for the Armenian question during Nero's principate, see note on 13.1 above. In 61 both Parthian and Roman troops had been withdrawn from Armenia to give an opportunity for further negotiations. For reasons unknown they broke down and the Parthians resumed operations in Armenia in 62. Meantime Corbulo's command had at his own request been divided and, while he looked after Syria, Armenia was allotted to Caesennius Paetus. The latter was besieged by the Parthians at Rhandeia, to the north of the river Arsenias, and lost his nerve just when the Parthians were on the point of giving up. A truce was concluded on the basis of another Roman withdrawal. Tacitus (*Ann.* 15.15.2) shows that the withdrawal took place under humiliating circumstances but says, undoubtedly correctly, that it was only a rumour that legions had been sent 'under the yoke'. As for Suetonius' assertion that Syria had only been held with difficulty, this too is incorrect; Corbulo had marshalled his army on the Euphrates and also had a bridgehead across it, and Vologaeses never attacked Syria at all. See Warmington (1969) 90ff.

mirum et vel praecipue...exstitisse: this point and the examples which illustrate it really form a sort of appendix to the list of Nero's crimes. Although it seems to be at variance with the statement in 32.2, it may perhaps be accepted in that jokes or abuse from anonymous or unimportant people were one thing, especially if made in the theatre where some licence was allowed, whereas hostile remarks by politically important senators were another. In any case there was little Nero could do about anonymous *graffiti*.

39.2
Νέρων...etc.: this line is quoted by Dio (61.16.2) with the last word in the plural:

'Nero, Orestes, Alcmaeon, all matricides'. The singular may also be correct; Vindex (see 40.1 below) is given a speech by Dio (63.22.6), in which he says that Nero should not have the names Caesar and Augustus but Thyestes and Oedipus, or Orestes and Alcmaeon. The line would thus mean 'Nero Orestes Alcmaeon is a matricide'. νεόψηφον...etc.: 'a new calculation; Nero killed his mother'. Apparently the numerical value of the Greek letters in Νέρων equals the value of the letters in the rest of the sentence; see note in the Loeb edition.

sustulit hic matrem: *tollere* has a double meaning.

dum tendit citharam...ille Hecatebeletes: another elaborate word play; 'while our ruler tunes his *cithara* and the Parthian bends his bow, ours will be (Apollo) Paean, theirs (Apollo) Hecatebeletes'. Paean gives the meaning of Apollo the musician, Hecatebeletes Apollo as a warrior-archer.

Roma domus...ista domus: the reference is to the Golden House. Veii lay the other side of the Tiber.

quosdam per indicem...poena prohibuit: probably generalising from a single instance. In 62 the *praetor* Antistius Sosianus was charged in the senate with publishing offensive verses against Nero. Largely owing to the influence of Thrasea Paetus, the senate voted for exile rather than the death penalty; Nero said he would have reduced the extreme penalty anyway (Tacitus, *Ann.* 14.48-49).

Isidorus Cynicus: not otherwise known. A traditional feature of the Cynic philosphers was their outspokenness, which rulers were expected to tolerate even if it involved verbal abuse.

Naupli: Nauplius was a descendant of Poseidon and father of Palamedes; in the late epic, Palamedes was a rival of Odysseus in cunning but was framed by the latter on a charge of treason and put to death by the Greeks. To avenge him Nauplius lit false beacons on Euboea to wreck the Greek fleet on its return. The theme was also treated in Euripides' lost play *Palamedes* (burlesqued in Aristophanes' *Thesmophoriazusae*). It presumably played a part in Nero's *Troica*.

datus Atellanarum histrio: the so-called Atellan farce derived its name from the Oscan town of Atella. With stock characters, broad humour (often political) and everyday language these farces were extremely popular in the late Republic and early principate.

ὑγίαινε πάτερ...etc.:   'Goodbye father, goodbye mother'.

Orcus vobis ducit pedes: Orcus, the god of the underworld. The reference was to Nero's threat in 37.3.

histrionem et philosophum...summovit: Nero's reaction to Datus' joke compares favourably with that of Gaius (*Caligula* 27.4) and Domitian (*Domitian* 10). Isidorus was not the only philosopher exiled under Nero; others were Demetrius, another Cynic and friend of Thrasea Paetus, and the Stoics Annaeus Cornutus and Musonius Rufus; all appear to have been exiled in 65 or after.

40.1
Suetonius formally announces the fall of Nero, as if what follows is a sort of set piece. Reference has been made to the effectiveness of this account. However, Baldwin (1983) 175 and others have remarked upon the implausibilities of the narrative, and also, having regard to similarities with Dio, considered whether there was a single source for it.

talem principem...tandem destituit: The account of Nero's fall can be supplemented by Dio, 63.22ff., which has major similarities, by Plutarch's *Galba* and Suetonius' own *Galba*. The loss of Tacitus for this extremely important event is most regrettable since many difficulties and uncertainties remain. From the point of view of historical knowledge Suetonius' view of what was biographically relevant is here most frustrating, as he limits himself almost entirely to Nero's reactions to the situation; in biography this is reasonable to a degree except that the stages of the unfolding crisis are given in only the vaguest outline. The whole story was also no doubt the subject of deliberate obscuration under the Flavian emperors since it was in the interest of many important figures to claim early defection from Nero: see Syme (1958) 179. The most reasonable reconstruction of the events is by Brunt (1959) 531ff.; see also Chilver (1957) and Hainsworth (1962).

initium facientibus Gallis: the superficially attractive idea that the revolt of Vindex (see below) was really an attempt by the Gauls (or some of them) to obtain independence from the Roman Empire is decisively countered by Brunt (1959). Although most sources, like Suetonius, make the point that it was the Gauls who began the revolt, there is no evidence to indicate that Vindex and his immediate associates, romanised Gallic notables, had any motive other than the overthrow of Nero as emperor, and there is much to support this latter interpretation. The extent of Vindex' immediate support is not known; we hear of the Aedui,

Arverni and Sequani, significantly perhaps the most important Gallic *civitates* close to the centre of events. The *colonia* Vienna (Vienne) in Gallia Narbonensis supported Vindex, but Lugdunum, although it was the capital of the province of which he was governor, remained loyal to Nero out of gratitude for his assistance after the city had been damaged by fire.

Iulio Vindice: C. Julius Vindex was a descendent of tribal kings in Aquitania; his family's citizenship presumably goes back to Caesar or Augustus and his father benefited from Claudius' admission of some Gauls to a senatorial career. At the time of his revolt he was *legatus Aug. pro praetore* apparently of Gallia Lugdunensis, regarded as the Gallic province *par excellence (eam provinciam)*. Aquitania and Belgica seem to be excluded on various grounds; see Brunt (1959). One most important point was that he had no troops at his disposal (nor for that matter did any of the governors of the Gallic provinces); further, his own rank (praetorian), lack of a distinguished social origin as Romans understood it, and still more (at this date) his provincial origin made it impossible for him to seek to have himself made emperor. He therefore contacted other governors to see if they would join a revolt against Nero, including, it must be presumed, those nearest to him in Upper and Lower Germany. All except Galba informed Nero of his approach and Vindex was thus forced to rebel in spite of almost complete lack of support. He claimed to have 100,000 followers but the losses when his army was annihilated are only put at 20,000; see Plutarch, *Galba* 4ff. and Dio, 63.22. The revolt began in early March 68.

40.2

praedictum a mathematicis...destitueretur: the astrologers (*mathematici*), most, though not all, of whom came from the eastern provinces were repeatedly both believed and feared by the emperors and from time to time were expelled from Italy (e.g. *Tiberius* 36) but constantly returned; for Balbillus advising Nero, see 36.1 above.

τὸ τέχνον ἡμᾶς διατρέφει: 'my art will support me'. This celebrated remark is placed by Dio (63.27.2) after Galba had joined Vindex, but Suetonius clearly had in mind an earlier occasion (*olim*).

spoponderant tamen...regnum Hierosolymorum: the implications of these remarkable prophecies are considerable. The former in general terms can be associated with the détente reached with the Parthians and the popularity enjoyed by Nero in the Greek world (see 57 below) since it is rule over the eastern parts of the empire rather than areas still farther east which are in view, but in fact the two ideas are connected and based upon a widespread acceptance among the urban poor in the East, from which the prophecies certainly came, of a belief in an apocalyptic reversal of the existing order, which in turn derived from the Jews' Messianic hope. The idea of Nero as Messiah seems preposterous, but *regnum Hierosolymorum* is specific and the prevalence of the Messianic idea at precisely this time is confirmed from Roman sources by *Vespasian* 4.5: *percrebuerat Oriente toto vetus et constans opinio esse in fatis ut eo tempore Iudaea profecti rerum potirentur;* the prophecy was applied (with success) to Vespasian in 69. That up to 66 some Jews might regard Nero favourably is confirmed by Josephus (*A.J.* 20.8.11), though of course Suetonius does not say that the prophecy comes directly from Jews. For the frequency of Jewish embassies to Rome see Millar (1977) 376ff.; there was there, as everywhere, an interest in Jewish religion. Note Pliny, *N.H.* 5.70, where he calls Jerusalem *longe clarissima urbium Orientis, non Iudaeae modo,* which is remarkable, considering the importance of Antioch and Alexandria.

Britannia Armeniaque amissa: Suetonius, Dio (62.1.1) and Tacitus (*Agricola* 16) agree in regarding Britain as actually or potentially lost to Rome during the revolt of Boudicca; see Warmington (1976) 47. Armenia could be regarded as lost through the humiliation at Rhandeia (39.1 above) and recovered through the investiture of Tiridates.

40.3
septuagesimum ac tertium annum: this is incorrect since Galba was only 71 in 68; see Gallivan (1974) 305.

40.4
Neapoli...occiderat: the death of Agrippina had been towards the end of March; this information effectively dates the revolt of Vindex to early March.

adeoque lente...obliteravit: almost identical in Dio (63.36.1), who says Nero received the news at the gymnastic contest just after luncheon. Naturally the real reason for Nero's complacency was the fact that Vindex had no legionary forces at his disposal, and his rapid suppression by the Rhine legions must have seemed a foregone conclusion, especially if, as seems probable, the commanders had already informed Nero of Vindex' disaffection.

41.1
edictis tandem...appellatum: for Nero's sore throat, see Dio, 63.26.1. On the use of Nero's original name as a form of abuse after his death by the Elder Pliny,

see 7.1 above. There is no reason to doubt that Vindex' propaganda contained the sort of abuse referred to here. Dio (63.22.11) gives Vindex a speech to the Gauls at the outset of the revolt containing in extended form what Suetonius summarises from the proclamations. Although the speech was doubtless Dio's own construction, following the usual ancient historiographical practice, it probably had a basis in references from his sources to such edicts. The sort of abuse specified was obviously calculated to appeal to increasingly disgruntled elements, especially among the soldiers and their commanders.

41.2

sed urgentibus aliis...praetrepidus rediit: the time of Nero's return to Rome is not certain but was presumably in early April. Suetonius may well have exaggerated Nero's alarm at this stage, but he would no doubt have been concerned that the expected rapid annihilation of Vindex' inexperienced levies had not happened.

ac ne tunc quidem...cuiusque disserens: this item on a meeting of the *consilium principis* which is what is implied by *quosdam e primoribus viris domum evocavit*, and an inspection of a water organ (plural in Suetonius) is similar in Dio (63.26.4). It was of course quite natural for Nero to call his *consilium* in an emergency rather than to address the senate and people. For Suetonius' *primores* Dio has 'the most important senators and knights (i.e. *equites*)'.

42.1

postquam deinde etiam Galbam...cognovit: Galba received a letter from Vindex urging him 'to be the champion of the human race' (*Galba* 9.2) at the end of March when he was at Carthago Nova (Cartagena), about the same time as he received a letter from the governor of Aquitania asking him to help put down the rebellion; see Plutarch, *Galba* 4-5. Servius Sulpicius Galba was a member of an old Republican family and had had an exceptionally distinguished career from Tiberius onwards. He had been consul in 33, legate of Upper Germany and pro-consul of Africa. His appointment as *legatus* of Hispania Tarraconensis in 60 and his long tenure of the post indicate both Nero's confidence in his loyalty and also his own addiction to holding office, since he was now exceptionally old for the task, and the post ranked lower in status than those he had already held. His acceptance of Vindex' plea is said to have been determined by his interception of messages from Nero instructing his procurators to kill him. Perhaps Nero suspected that Galba had treasonably failed to denounce an approach by Vindex. Galba refused to proclaim himself emperor but threw off his allegiance to Nero and styled himself *legatus* of the Senate and Roman people, hoping no doubt by this gesture to win senatorial support; the date was 2 April. See Dio, 64.6.52 and

63.23; Plutarch, *Galba*, 5.2 and 22.2; Suetonius, *Galba* 10. Though initially joined by Otho, *legatus* of Lusitania, and Caecina, quaestor of Baetica (hence Suetonius' *Hispanias*), he had only one legion at his disposal. Allowing a minimum of a week for the news to reach Rome, Nero would have heard it on 9 April; see Gallivan (1974) 315.

consolantique...memoranti: see 50 below for two of Nero's nurses. The remark of one of them in this instance was meant to be encouraging though it was hardly exact; only one rebellion by a provincial governor had taken place before this, that of L. Arruntius Scribonianus, *legatus* of Dalmatia, against Claudius in 42; it had lasted only four days.

42.2

cum prosperi quiddam...nuntiatum esset: not apparently any major event such as the destruction of Vindex' army; the point is to bring out Nero's alternating moods of despair and euphoria.

43.1

initio statim...defenderentur: some of these alleged plans are placed by Dio (63.27.2) after the revolt of Galba; but *initio tumultus* ought to mean the revolt of Vindex. However, the list is undoubtedly a compilation made up from rumours circulating at various times in Nero's last months or even after his death and it is difficult to believe that they had much basis in fact. To replace some army commanders might be reasonable, if it could be done without provoking them into joining the rebellion, but to send assassins looks reminiscent of the report of the orders intercepted by Galba.

43.2

credensque expeditionem...nisi a consule: Nero's assumption of the sole consulship appears to have taken place in the middle of April since the whole section assumes that Vindex was still in arms. The assumption of a sole consulship was a symbolic reaction to crisis.

Suetonius alone reports the projected *expeditio* to Gaul which he was to lead in person, and the details look unconvincing, again being part of the picture of Nero's hopelessly emotional and impractical attitude in the final crisis. Some sensible measures were in fact taken after Galba's defection was known; legions were summoned from Illyricum and units assembling or on their way east for the Caspian expedition were recalled (Tacitus, *Hist.* 1.6.9, 31 and 70); see also *Hist.* 4.74, though how many had mustered in Italy by the time of Nero's death in early June is not clear. Forces already available were put under the command of two distinguished men of consular rank, Rubrius Gallus and Petronius Turpilianus (Dio, 63.27.1); the latter had been governor of Britain from 61 to 63.

44.1
mox tribus urbanas...recepit: nothing else is known of this; a mobilisation of the city populace at this date would hardly have produced satisfactory recruits; slaves enrolled would have been freed first. Augustus himself had been driven to raise forced levies and freed slaves after the disaster in Germany in 9. Not mentioned by Suetonius (but otherwise known) is the *Legio I Adiutrix* recruited from the fleet at Misenum.

45.1
ex annonae quoque...advexisse: it is not clear how Nero had been profiting from the cost of grain. A *publica fames* could have been caused by the diversion of stocks of grain for the army assembling in northern Italy. Pliny (*N.H.* 35.168) refers to Patrobius, a freedman of Nero, transporting sand from Egypt for use on the exercise grounds, and this may be the incident Suetonius refers to. If the price of grain was rising no doubt popular opinion blamed the government; Suetonius is in fact contradicted by Tacitus (*Hist.* 1.89), who says that in 69, when Otho prepared to fight Vitellius, the masses in Rome were affected by the trouble for the first time: *conversa in militum usum omni pecunia, intentis alimentorum pretiis quae motu Vindicis haud perinde plebem attriverant.* See K.R. Bradley, *American Journal of Philology* 93 (1972) 451ff.

45.2
quare omnium: The examples of *graffiti* accord with the Roman traditions of popular abuse even if the full flavour is lost.

nunc demum...traderet tandem: the first words seem represent the colloquial Greek νῦν γὰρ ἐστιν ἄγων, 'now is the time for action' but there is a pun: a common meaning of ἄγων is a contest in Greek festivals; Nero is apparently to lose at last.

alterius collo...meruisti: the word *ascopera*, only here in Latin, is the Greek ασκοπήρα, a sort of knapsack. Perhaps the reference is to the death of Agrippina. Nero says 'What else could I do?', the answer being, 'Whatever, you deserve the sack'. The penalty for parricide was to be tied in a sack (*culleum*) and thrown into the sea.

etiam Gallos...excitasse: obvious punning, Galli means either 'Gauls' or 'cocks'.

iam noctibus...poscebant: another pun, this time on the name Vindex, which means 'champion' or 'liberator'. Suetonius would not know that Vindex is a Latinised form of a Celtic name with the root *vind-* meaning 'white' and common in Celtic place names (e.g. Vindolanda, Vindobona).

46.1
asturco: a favoured breed of horse from Asturia.

46.2
Mausoleo: the Mausoleum of Augustus, in which, however, Nero was not buried; see 50 below. Dio (63.26.5) has this omen and some others not listed by Suetonius; the fall of Nero clearly provoked a large number of such tales.

Kal. Ian....conciderunt: the *Lares Praestites*, tutelary *Lares* of the city of Rome are meant. On 1 January each year oaths of allegiance were sworn. The date would presumably be the first day of 68.

auspicanti Sporus...raptus: the omen being that Proserpina had been dragged off to Hades by Pluto.

votorum nuncupatione: on 3 January each year vows were made for the safety of the emperor.

46.3
θανεῖν...πάτηρ: 'wife, mother and father drive me to my death'. Dio (63.28.5) quotes the line somewhat differently and says it was constantly running through Nero's mind.

47.1
nuntiata interim...defectione: the only army whose defection has so far been implied, not stated, by Suetonius is that of Galba, and he here goes directly from the assumption of the sole consulship in mid-April to Nero's last few days in early June. A crucial event had occurred in early May. Vindex had been besieging Lugdunum, which was loyal to Nero, when Verginius Rufus, legate of Upper Germany, marched with three legions against Vesontio (Besançon) which was in the hands of the rebels. What happened then is obscure; according to Dio (63.24.1) the two leaders had a secret meeting and came to an agreement but a battle took place through a misunderstanding in which the rebel force of 20,000 was annihilated and Vindex committed suicide. It is more than likely that aggressive desire for plunder on the part of the legionaries, who could feel totally

confident in the outcome of a battle, played a part; their plundering instincts were demonstrated several times in the civil wars of 69. On the other hand, it is notable that Rufus, whose forces were based only a few days march from the main rebel area, had taken so long to act; it is known that he called for legionary detachments and auxiliaries from his colleague in Lower Germany which may indicate a desire to build up a totally overwhelming force, but it is possible that he temporised as long as he dared to see if Vindex' rebellion would make progress elsewhere. After the battle (again according to Dio) Rufus was hailed as emperor by his troops but refused and persuaded them to abide by the choice of the Senate and People of Rome; Plutarch (*Galba* 6.1) implies that this had already happened before the battle. The matter is uncertain since later it was in the interest of Rufus and others to claim early defection from Nero. Rufus was not of distinguished social origin and presumably felt unable to accept the imperial position himself; his reference to the Senate and People of Rome would imply his acquiescence in their likely choice of Galba. On the news of the death of Vindex, Galba assumed that all was lost and fled to the interior of Spain; he could hardly know that Rufus would consistently refuse the imperial position himself, even if we assume that Dio's date for Rufus' defection from Nero is correct, and it is known that the legions on the Rhine were reluctant to accept Galba to the end.

Of the other provinces, Plutarch (*Galba* 6.1) says that at the time of the battle at Vesontio many were falling away from Nero and supporting Galba. In North Africa a former mistress of Nero had instigated Clodius Macer, legate of the *Legio III Augusta* to rebel; like Galba and Rufus he professed allegiance to the senate but in fact operated on his own account and was easily removed later by Galba; see Plutarch, *Galba* 6.1 and Tacitus, *Hist.* 1.7.73. It also seems likely that the prefect of Egypt, Ti. Julius Alexander, had reached an understanding with Galba before Nero's death. The Illyrian legions had also made overtures to Rufus (Tacitus, *Hist.* 1.9.2); see Brunt (1959) 541. It may also be that Rubrius Gallus defected, though Petronius Turpilianus remained loyal to the end and was executed by Galba (Tacitus, *Hist.* 1.6; Plutarch, *Galba* 15.17). Thus Nero's last hope remained in reaching the eastern provinces; hence his attempt to get to Ostia. And it is not surprising that Tacitus (*Hist.* 1.89) could depict Nero as *nuntiis magis et rumoribus quam armis depulsus.* These developments, however obscure in detail, are eloquent testimony of the hatred and contempt now felt for Nero by the upper classes of Roman society who provided the provincial governors and the officers in the army, who showed total unwillingness to fight for him.

mensam subvertit: see also Plutarch (*Galba* 5), who, however, puts this after the defection of Galba.

Suetonius: Nero

duos scyphos...inlisit: similar in Pliny, *N.H.* 37.29.

tribunos centurionesque praetorii...temptavit: a crucial factor in the downfall of Nero was the attitude of the praetorian guard. In spite of the defections in the provinces, nothing could be done at Rome while the guard remained loyal to Nero. The sources tell us nothing of the activities of one of the two praetorian prefects, Ofonius Tigellinus, who had been appointed after the death of Burrus and who is given an extremely bad character by Tacitus; he had played a major part in suppressing the Pisonian conspiracy, in which his colleague Faenius Rufus had been implicated. Tigellinus is also described as the *desertor ac proditor* of Nero but he was put to death by Galba nevertheless (Tacitus, *Hist.* 1.72). Faenius Rufus was replaced by Nymphidius Sabinus, who appears to have been the more decisive in the crisis of 68; it was probably he who arranged with the senate to induce the guard to desert Nero, and on the night of 8/9 June when Nero fled from Rome he went with senators to the praetorian camp and, after telling the soldiers that Nero had fled and promising a large donative, persuaded them to proclaim Galba as emperor (Dio, 64.3.3 and 63.27.2). The hesitation of the tribunes and centurions in this passage indicates that they knew something was in the wind and had no confidence that Nero could do anything to re-establish his position even if he got to Ostia and thence to the East. Note that in the Pisonian conspiracy, in addition to the prefect Faenius Rufus, 3 of the 16 tribunes had been implicated and 4 more were discharged afterwards.

47.2
usque adeo...miserum est: quotation from Virgil, *Aen.* 12.646.

Aegypti praefecturam: perhaps an aspect of the rumour that he intended to flee to Alexandria (Dio, 63.27.2; Plutarch, *Galba* 17).

47.3
stationem militum recessisse: i.e. the cohort on duty at the palace.

spiculum: see 30.2 above.

48.1
The narrative of Nero's last few hours in sections 48 and 49 is similar to that in Dio, 63.27.3-29.2; no doubt the source is the same, the differences being largely due to Suetonius' total concentration – here very effective – on Nero's actions while Dio has rhetorical devices of a more commonplace character to try to make more dramatic what was already dramatic enough.

84

offerente Phaonte liberto...equum inscendit: Phaon was *a rationibus*; see Millar (1977) 77. The escape route looks incredibly hazardous. The *via Salaria* and *via Nomentana* were in the opposite direction from Ostia, to which one might suppose Nero would still hope to get. Whether Nero were to leave the city by the *Porta Salaria* or the *Porta Nomentana*, he would pass extremely close to the praetorian camp, and it is not surprising that he could hear the soldiers shouting for Galba (see section 48.2 below). This is one of the items in the story of Nero's last hours which suggests disloyalty among the imperial freedmen as well as among other groups; on this possibility, see Townend (1967) 95. They might perhaps hope to save their own lives by ensuring that he committed suicide and by claiming credit for preventing him from escaping to the East.

48.3
haec est Neronis decocta: see also Dio, 63.28.5. According to Pliny (*N.H.* 31.40) Nero invented the practice of having water boiled, then chilled by being plunged into the snow in a glass vessel. *aqua* is to be understood with *decocta*.

49.1
qualis artifex pereo: Dio (63.29.2) dramatically makes these Nero's last words as he stabbed himself.

ἵππων...βάλλει: Homer, *Iliad* 10.535: 'the thunder of swift horses strikes on my ears'.

Epaphrodito a libellis: he had perhaps held the post at least since 65 (Tacitus, *Ann.* 15.55.1). He is known to have survived Nero's death but was later exiled by Domitian and executed in 95 (Dio, 67.14.4-5).

50.1
funeratus est: The funerals or disposal of the bodies of all emperors are recorded by Suetonius. In spite of all the circumstances of his death, at least as detailed in the narrative, and Nero's unpopularity with the Roman and Italian upper classes, his body was not treated with the indignity inflicted on other emperors' (*Caligula* 59, *Galba* 20, *Vitellius* 17, *Domitian* 17). Presumably the credit for the honourable treatment goes to Galba or his freedman Icelus. However, the burial in the family tomb of the Domitii symbolically removed him from the Julian and Claudian families, and thus compliments the emphasis on Nero as a Domitius with which Suetonius had begun the *Life*.

51.1

ter omnino...languit: Tacitus (*Ann.* 14.22.6) mentions an illness in 60.

synthesinam: *vestem* is to be understood; a highly coloured robe worn at dinner at the Saturnalia; Dio (63.13.3) says it had a floral pattern and also mentions Nero wearing a neck cloth and appearing in public in an ungirded tunic. The hair style described by Suetonius appears on Nero's image on the coinage from 64 onwards (*BMC* 1.clxv).

52.1

liberalis disciplinas...contrariam esse: Nero had naturally received the formal education of a Roman noble until he became emperor. In a passage curiously similar Tacitus (*Agricola* 4) says that his father-in-law Agricola had when young been addicted to philosophy 'more than was fitting for a Roman and a senator' and been rescued by his mother, and Seneca too had been warned against too much enthusiasm for the subject. The reason was not so much that the study might lead to subversive ideas (at least in Nero's case), but the more conventional one that philosophy was regarded by the average Roman mind as a hindrance to an active political life; see also Tacitus, *Ann.* 13.42.4.

a cognitione...detineret: the story assumes that Nero would have preferred the older orators to Seneca, which seems at best dubious since he was nothing if not up to date. Suetonius seems here to follow a tradition hostile to Seneca which is found in reference to other matters in Dio, though not in Tacitus.

itaque ad poeticam...inerant: Nero wrote verses as part of his education and Tacitus (*Ann.* 13.3.5) says they had some merit, but his enthusiasm for poetry appears to date from 59 (*Ann.* 14.16.1-8). The passage in Suetonius is often said to indicate that he read Tacitus' work since he seems to be quietly contradicting what Tacitus says in the last mentioned reference: *carminum quoque studium adfectavit, contractis quibus aliqua pangendi facultas necdum insignis erat. hi cenati considere simul et adlatos vel ibidem repertos versus connectere atque ipsius verba quoquo modo prolata supplere, quod species ipsa carminum docet, non impetu et instinctu nec ore uno fluens.* However, Suetonius' description of the heavily corrected manuscripts does not disprove Tacitus' allegation of composite poems put together at sessions after dinner; if anything they could be taken to confirm it, especially as there is no suggestion in Tacitus of dictation or a fair copy. We have only a few verses by Nero, insufficient to say whether Tacitus' judgement, based purely on stylistic grounds, is justified, but Nero is not otherwise accused of plagiarism, and the fact that he wrote (or planned) works of epic proportions suggests that he had a certain facility. Nero's works included an epic on Troy, normally referred to as the *Troica* (Dio, 62.29.1; Scholiast on Persius, 1.121; Servius on Virgil, *Georgic* 3.36 and *Aeneid* 5.370), though the *Halosis Ilii* referred to in 38.2 above and in Tacitus, *Ann.* 15.39 (*Troianum excidium*) was probably part of it. He also wrote hymns (Tacitus, *Ann.* 15.34) and erotic poetry (Pliny, *N.H.* 37.50; Martial, 9.26.9); satires are also referred to (24.2 above; *Domitian* 1.1; Tacitus, *Ann.* 15.49). For a projected epic on Rome, see Dio, 62.29.2.

habuit et pingendi...non mediocre studium: see also Tacitus, *Ann.* 13.3.7.

53.1

proximo lustro: at the next celebration of the Olympic Games which would be in 69. The implication is that Nero had developed yet another enthusiasm, wrestling, and would now compete among the athletes, as if his competing as a charioteer and *citharoedus* were not disgraceful enough.

54.1

sunt qui...adversarium: see also Dio, 63.18.1.

55.1

erat illi...Neropolim nuncupare: the month April was named Neroneus in 65 (Tacitus, *Ann.* 15.74.1); the same year a further decree made May into Claudius and June into Germanicus (*Ann.* 16.12.3). For Nero's wish to name Rome after himself, see Tacitus, *Ann.* 15.40.3. Artaxata and Caesarea Philippi were both named Neronias (Dio, 63.7.2; Josephus, *A.J.* 20.211).

56.1

deae Syriae: i.e. Atargatis or *Magna Mater*, widely worshipped in the eastern provinces.

57.1

obiit tricensium...interemerat: Nero's death was on 9 June 68; see Gallivan (1974) 318.

et tamen...in rostris proferrent: there is no reason to doubt this. Tacitus (*Hist.* 1.4-5) says that 'the base plebs, addicted to the circus and the theatre' were resentful at Nero's death. In 69 Otho found it worthwhile to try to win some popular following by associating himself with the memory of Nero instead of with the unpopular Galba and he is said even to have issued edicts using the name

Nero (*Otho* 7.10; Tacitus, *Hist.* 1.78; Plutarch, *Otho* 3). Vitellius also used the same tactic (*Vitellius* 11, Tacitus, *Hist.* 2.71.95; Dio, 65.7.3).

at brevi magno...malo reversuri: belief that Nero was not truly dead and would return is attested by the appearances of 'false Neros' and by other evidence. It was primarily current in the East (Dio Chrysostom, *Orations* 31.9 and 10). It entered Jewish and then early Christian apocalyptic writing, where Nero's return as the precursor of Antichrist at the end of the world is prophesied. See Warmington (1969) 168 and Charlesworth (1950).

quin etiam...memoria coleretur: the relationship established between Rome and Parthia by Nero is viewed as an alliance; because of the circumstances of the death of Nero it must have seemed essential to the Parthians to renew it. Vologaeses reigned until 79 or 80 but the embassy no doubt came early in Vespasian's principate.

denique cum post...redditus sit: no less than three pretenders claiming to be Nero appeared within a generation of his death; the first was in 69 when a slave or freedman seized the island of Cythnos and rumours about the event caused alarm in Achaia and Asia (Tacitus, *Hist.* 2.8). Under Titus, probably in 80, another appeared in Asia Minor and gathered some followers before crossing into Parthia, where he was received by a pretender to the Parthian throne but nothing significant occurred. The third, referred to by Suetonius, appeared in 88-89. Tacitus (*Hist.* 1.2.1) seems to refer to trouble with the Parthians over this incident; see also Statius, *Silvae* 4.3.107-110. What real reason the Parthians had for supporting a false Nero at this time is not known, but their action did not lead to open war. See Gallivan (1973) 364-365.